STREET GERMAN-1
THE BEST OF GERMAN IDIOMS

To order the accompanying cassette for

STREET GERMAN-1

See the coupon on the last page for details

STREET GERMAN-1
THE BEST OF GERMAN IDIOMS

David Burke

Publisher: Optima Books
Editing, Design, and Production: Optima PrePress
Front Cover Illustration: Ty Semaka
Inside Illustrations: Ty Semaka

Library of Congress Cataloging-in-Publication Data
Burke, David
     Street German -1: The Best of German Idioms / David Burke
          p.   cm.
     ISBN 1-879440-21-0
     1. German language—Idioms.   2. German language—Slang.
     3. German
     language—Textbooks for foreign speakers—English.   I. Title
     PF3460.B87   1994
     438.3'421—dc20   95-24216
                                                                   CIP

Printed in the United States of America
10 9 8 7 6 5 4 3 2 1

This book is dedicated to Stefan, Anne, and Cassady.

Introduction

To the outsider, idioms seem like a confusing "secret" code reserved only for the native speaker of German. Idioms are certainly tricky beasts because it is the *sum* of all the words in the phrase which must be interpreted, not each word by itself. In other words, the listener must never confuse the literal translation of an idiom with the underlying meaning of what is really being expressed or symbolized. In English, if you are told *"Get me a pizza... and step on it!"* you are not being instructed to go trample on a round piece of cheesy bread. You are simply being told to hurry, since *"step on it"* refers to "pressing down on" the accelerator of a car.

In German, a common idiom such as *"Hühnchen mit jemandem zu rupfen haben (ein)"* (colloquial meaning: "to have a bone to pick with someone" • literal meaning: "to have a chicken to pluck with someone") has nothing to do with preparing for a meal. It's simply a colorful way of conveying anger toward someone.

> example: Mit der **hab ich auch noch ein Hühnchen zu rupfen**!

> translation: I have a bone to pick with her!

> literal translation: I have a chicken to pluck with her!

In short, idioms are simply an imaginative and expressive way to communicate an idea or thought. In order to be considered proficient in German, idioms must be learned since they are consistently used in books, magazines, television, movies, songs, German homes, etc.

Learning the information in **STREET GERMAN -1** will equal years of living in Germany and reduce the usual time it takes to absorb the intricacies of slang and colloquialisms.

STREET GERMAN -1 is a self-teaching guide made up of ten chapters, each divided into four primary parts:

■ **DIALOGUE**

Ten to fifteen popular German idioms (indicated in boldface) are presented as they may be heard in an actual conversation. A translation of the dialogue in standard English is always given on the opposite page. The third page is an entertaining literal translation of the opening dialogue.

■ **VOCABULARY**

This section spotlights all of the idioms that were used in the dialogue and offers examples of usage for each entry, including synonyms and special notes.

■ **PRACTICE THE VOCABULARY**

These word games include all of the idioms previously learned and will help you to test yourself on your comprehension. *(The pages providing the answers to all the drills are indicated at the beginning of this section.)*

■ **DICTATION (Test your oral comprehension)**

Using an optional audio cassette *(see coupon on back page),* the student will hear a paragraph containing many of the idioms from the opening dialogue.

At the end of each five chapters is a review exam encompassing all of the words and expressions learned up to that point.

If you have always prided yourself on being fluent in German, you will undoubtedly be surprised and amused to encounter a whole new world of phrases usually hidden away in the German language and reserved only for the native speaker...*until now!*

David Burke
Author

Acknowledgments

I owe an enormous debt of gratitude to Stefan and Anne Kloo for all of their hard work and significant contribution toward this book. Their insight into the *real* German language was indespensible. I'm thankful for having the chance to work with them and especially grateful for their friendship.

I am, once again, very thankful to Ty Semaka, our illustrator and cover artist. His creativity and ability to produce exceptional images is always astounding.

I'm grateful to Douglas Werner for his contribution in this project as proofreader. His enthusiasm and keen eye are highly regarded.

A very special thanks to Joachim Winterhalder for making the copy-editing phase of this book so enjoyable. His expertise, professionalism, and attitude are greatly appreciated.

Legend

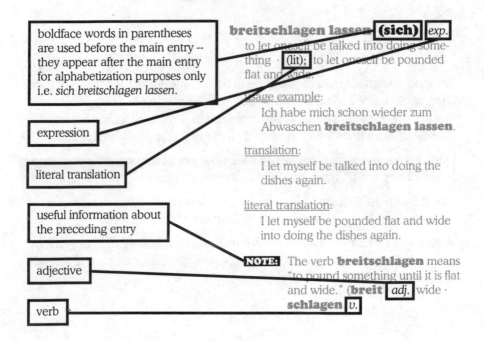

boldface words in parentheses are used before the main entry -- they appear after the main entry for alphabetization purposes only i.e. *sich breitschlagen lassen*.

expression

literal translation

useful information about the preceding entry

adjective

verb

breitschlagen lassen (sich) *exp.*
to let oneself be talked into doing something · **(lit);** to let oneself be pounded flat and wide.

usage example:
Ich habe mich schon wieder zum Abwaschen **breitschlagen lassen**.

translation:
I let myself be talked into doing the dishes again.

literal translation:
I let myself be pounded flat and wide into doing the dishes again.

NOTE: The verb **breitschlagen** means "to pound something until it is flat and wide." (**breit** *adj.* wide · **schlagen** *v.*

Contents

Preface vii

Acknowledgements ix

Legend x

Lesson 1   1

In der Schule
At School

Dialogues 2

Vocabulary 5

Practice the Vocabulary 11

Lesson 2   17

Auf der Party
At the Party

Dialogues 18

Vocabulary 21

Practice the Vocabulary 28

Lesson 3   33

Der Hausgast
The House Guest

Dialogues 34

Vocabulary 37

Practice the Vocabulary 44

Lesson 4   49

Im Restaurant
At the Restaurant

Dialogues 50

Vocabulary 53

Practice the Vocabulary 60

Lesson 5   65

Am Strand
At the Beach

Dialogues 66

Vocabulary 69

Practice the Vocabulary 73

Review Exam for Lessons 1-5   79

Lesson 6   87

Im Supermarkt
At the Market

Dialogues 88
Vocabulary 91
Practice the Vocabulary 96

Lesson 7   101

Ein Skiausflug
A Ski Trip

Dialogues 102
Vocabulary 105
Practice the Vocabulary 110

Lesson 8   115

Im Einkaufszentrum
At the Mall

Dialogues 116
Vocabulary 119
Practice the Vocabulary 124

Lesson 9   129

Samstag Nacht
Saturday Night

Dialogues 130
Vocabulary 133
Practice the Vocabulary 139

Lesson 10   143

Im Nachtclub
At the Nightclub

Dialogues 144
Vocabulary 147
Practice the Vocabulary 151

Review Exam for Lessons 6-10   155

APPENDIX (Dictation)   174

GLOSSARY   179

"die beleidigte Leberwurst spielen"

(trans): to be in a huff
(lit): to play the pouting liverwurst

Dialogue in slang

In der Schule

Petra: Was ist dir nur für eine **Laus über die Leber gelaufen**, Anne? Warum **spielst du die beleidigte Leberwurst**?

Anne: Ich habe die Erdkundearbeit **in den Sand gesetzt**. Da habe ich mir wirklich **einen groben Schnitzer** erlaubt! Dabei dachte ich, ich kenne Europa **wie meine Westentasche**. Das hat mich wirklich **aus der Fassung gebracht**. Ich wußte, daß Frau Rater mich nicht mag.

Petra: Vielleicht hättest du doch besser zum Unterricht kommen sollen, anstatt ins Kino zu gehen.

Anne: Erdkunde **langweilt mich zu Tode**, und Frau Rater **geht mir so auf die Nerven**.

Petra: Na, **da liegt doch der Hund begraben**. Du kannst einfach unsere Lehrerin nicht leiden! Ich hoffe, du **kriegst das jetzt nicht in den falschen Hals**, aber wir sind schon so lange **ein Herz und eine Seele**, und ich weiß, daß ich ehrlich mit dir sein kann. Wenn du das nächste Mal eine Meinungsverschiedenheit mit Frau Rater hast, wäre es vielleicht besser, wenn du sie nicht vor der ganzen Klasse ein dummes **Miststück** nennen würdest. Ist ja nur so ein Vorschlag.

Lesson One

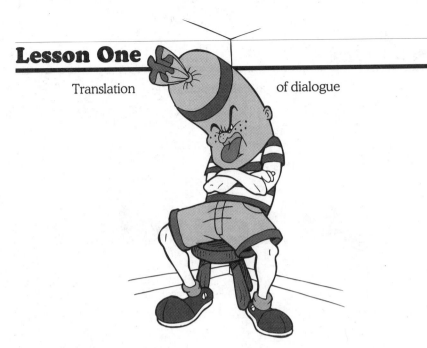

Translation of dialogue

Petra: **What's bugging you**, Anne? Why are you so **ticked off**?

Anne: I **failed** the geography test. I can't believe that I could **blow it** like this! I thought I knew Europe like the **back of my hand**. This really **threw me for a loop**. I knew that Mrs. Rater didn't like me.

Petra: Maybe you should have come to class yesterday instead of going to the movies.

Anne: Geography just **really bores me** and Mrs. Rater **gets on my nerves**.

Petra: Well, that's **the root of your problem**. You don't even like our teacher! I hope you don't **take this the wrong way**, but we're **great friends**, and I know I can be honest with you. Next time you don't agree with Mrs. Rater about something, it might be better if you didn't call her a **dirt bag** in front of the entire class. Just a suggestion...

Literal translation of dialogue

At School

Petra: What kind of **louse ran across your liver**, Anne? Why are you **playing the pouting Liverwurst**?

Anne: I **set the Geography test in the sand**. I really **allowed myself a bad woodcut** there. I thought I knew Europe **like my vest pocket**. This really brought me **out of composure**. I knew that Mrs. Rater didn't like me.

Petra: Maybe you should have come to class yesterday instead of going to the movies.

Anne: Geography just **bores me to death** and Mrs. Rater **gets on my nerves**.

Petra: Well, **that's where the dog lies buried**. You don't even like our teacher! I hope you don't get this **in the wrong throat**, but we're **one heart and one soul** for a long time now, and I know I can be honest with you. Next time you don't agree with Mrs. Rater about something, it might be better if you didn't call her a **dumb piece of manure** in front of the entire class. Just a suggestion...

Vocabulary

Fassung bringen (jemanden aus der) *exp.* to throw someone for a loop • (lit); to bring someone out of one's mounting or frame (in essence, composure).

usage example: Du hast mich völlig **aus der Fassung gebracht** mit deinen Bemerkungen über meine Figur!

translation: You really threw me for a loop with your remarks about my figure!

literal translation: You completely brought me out of composure with your remarks about my figure!

OTHER POPULAR IDIOMS USING "FASSUNG":

> **Fassung bewahren/verlieren** *exp.* to keep one's head • (lit); to keep/lose one's composure.

Hals kriegen (etwas in den falschen) *exp.* to take something the wrong way • (lit); to get something down the wrong throat.

usage example: Was ich über seine Frau gesagt habe, hat er völlig **in den falschen Hals gekriegt**.

translation: What I said about his wife, he completely took the wrong way.

literal translation: What I said about his wife, he really got down the wrong throat.

OTHER POPULAR IDIOMS USING "HALS":

> **aus vollem Halse lachen** *exp.* to roar with laughter • (lit); to laugh out of a full throat.
>
> **aus vollem Halse schreien** *exp.* to shout at the top of one's lungs • (lit); to yell out of a full throat.
>
> **Frosch im Hals haben (einen)** *exp.* to have a frog in one's throat • (lit); to have a frog in the throat.

Hals brechen (sich den) *exp.* to break one's neck • (lit); to break one's neck.

Hals umdrehen (jemandem den) *exp.* to wring someone's neck • (lit); to turn someone's neck around.

Kloß im Hals haben (einen) *exp.* to be speechless • (lit); to have a dumpling in the throat.

Herz und eine Seele sein (ein) *exp.* to be inseparable • (lit); to be one heart and one soul.

usage example: Es überrascht mich nicht, daß Kurt und Hanna heiraten. Sie waren schon immer **ein Herz und eine Seele** in der Schule.

translation: I'm not surprised that Kurt and Hanna are getting married. They were inseparable back in school.

literal translation: I'm not surprised that Kurt and Hanna are getting married. They were one heart and one soul back in school.

OTHER POPULAR IDIOMS USING "HERZ":

Hand aufs Herz! *exp.* Cross my heart! • (lit); hand on the heart.

Herzensbrecher *exp.* heart breaker • (lit); [same].

herzlos *exp.* heartless • (lit); heartless.

Herzschmerz *exp.* heartache • (lit); heart pain.

Herz auf der Zunge tragen *exp.* to wear one's heart on one's sleeve • (lit); to carry one's heart on the tongue.

Herzen gern (von) *exp.* from the bottom of my heart • (lit); with heart pleasure.

Herzen haben (etwas auf dem) *exp.* to have something on one's mind • (lit); to have something on one's heart.

Kind unter dem Herzen tragen (ein) *exp.* to be with child • (lit); to carry a child below the heart.

Mitten ins Herz *exp.* to be in love • (lit); right in the middle of the heart.

schweren Herzens *exp.* with a heavy heart • (lit); [same].

Stein fiel mir vom Herzen (ein) *exp.* to take a load off one's mind • (lit); a stone fell off my heart.

von ganzem Herzen *exp.* from the bottom of one's heart • (lit); from all of the heart.

Hund begraben (da liegt der) *exp.* to be the root of one's problem • (lit); that's where the dog lies buried.

usage example: Du nimmst immer Schmalz statt Butter?! Na, **da liegt doch der Hund begraben**. Deshalb werden deine Kuchen nichts.

translation: You're using lard instead of butter?! Well, there's your problem. That's why your cakes don't turn out.

literal translation: You're using lard instead of butter?! Well, there the dog lies buried. That's why your cakes don't turn out.

OTHER IDIOMS USING "HUND":

getroffene Hunde bellen *exp.* said of a guilty person who overacts his innocence • (lit); hit dogs bark.

Hundeleben (ein) *exp.* a dog's life • (lit); [same].

Hunde, die viel bellen, beißen nicht *exp.* Barking dogs seldom bite • (lit); dogs that bark a lot, don't bite.

Hundeelend sein *exp.* to be sick as a dog • (lit); [same].

Laus über die Leber gelaufen (jemandem ist eine) *exp.*
said of someone who is being bugged by something • (lit); someone had a louse run over his liver.

usage example: Lena hat den ganzen Tag noch nicht einmal gelächelt. Was ihr wohl für **eine Laus über die Leber gelaufen ist**?

translation: Lena didn't smile once all day. What's bugging her?

literal translation: Lena didn't smile once all day. What kind of louse ran across her liver?

OTHER IDIOMS USING "LAUS":

Laus in den Pelz setzen (jemandem eine) *exp.* to give someone problems • (lit); to put a louse in someone's fur.

OTHER IDIOMS USING "LEBER":

frei von der Leber weg reden *exp.* to speak one's mind • (lit); to talk freely from the liver.

Leberwurst spielen (die beleidigte) *exp.* to get in a huff • (lit); to play the pouting liverwurst.

usage example: Greta spielt **die beleidigte Leberwurst**, weil ich ihren Geburtstag vergessen habe.

translation: Greta is in a huff because I forgot her birthday.

literal translation: Greta is playing the offended liverwurst because I forgot her birthday.

Miststück *exp.* (insulting term used for especially for a woman) dirtbag • (lit); piece of manure.

usage example: Petra, dieses **Miststück**, hat mich beim Rektor verraten!

translation: Petra, that dirtbag, told the principal on me!

literal translation: Petra, that piece of manure, told the principal on me!

OTHER IDIOMS USING "MIST":

Misthaufen *exp.* pigsty • (lit); heap of manure.

Nerven gehen (jemandem auf die) *exp.* to annoy someone •
(lit); to go on one's nerves.

usage example: Das ist schon das fünfte Mal, daß du dasselbe Lied spielst.
Es geht mir **auf die Nerven**!

translation: That's the fifth time you've played the same song. It's
really bothering me!

literal translation: That's the fifth time you've played the same song. It goes
on my nerves!

OTHER IDIOMS USING "NERV" OR "NERVEN":

letzten Nerv rauben (jemandem den) *exp.* to
try one's patience • (lit); to steal someone's last
nerve.

Nerven haben *exp.* to have nerve • (lit); to have
nerves.

Nerven verlieren (die) *exp.* to lose one's temper
or to lose one's nerves • (lit); to lose the nerves.

Nerven wie Drahtseile haben *exp.* to have
nerves of steel • (lit); to have nerves like steel
cables.

Sand setzen (etwas in den) *exp.* to fail something miserably • (lit);
to set something in the sand.

usage example: Ich glaube, ich habe die Mathearbeit völlig **in den
Sand gesetzt**.

translation: I think I completely failed the math test.

literal translation: I think I really set the math test in the sand.

SYNONYM: **ein Griff ins Klo** exp. • (lit); grip into the toilet bowl.

OTHER IDIOMS USING "SAND":

Sande verlaufen (im) *exp.* to fizzle out • (lit); to
get lost in the sand.

Schnitzer machen (einen groben) *exp.* to make a big screw up, to blow it • (lit); to allow oneself a rough wood cut.

usage example: Da ist mir aber **ein grober Schnitzer** passiert, als ich versuchte, diese junge Frau auf der Party zu küssen. Es stellte sich heraus, daß es die Frau vom Chef war!

translation: I really blew it when I tried to kiss that young woman at the party. She turned out to be the boss's wife!

literal translation: I allowed myself a rough wood cut when I tried to kiss that young woman at the party. She turned out to be the boss's wife!

Tode langweilen (sich zu) *exp.* to bore one greatly • (lit); to bore one to death.

usage example: Ins Museum zu gehen, **langweilt mich zu Tode**.

translation: Going to museums bores me greatly!

literal translation: Going to museums bores me to death!

OTHER IDIOMS USING "TODE":

Tod holen (sich den) *exp.* to catch one's death • (lit); to get one's death.

Tod nicht leiden können (jemanden/etwas auf den) *exp.* to hate someone/something • (lit); not to be able to bear someone up to death.

Tod finden (den) *exp.* to meet one's death • (lit); to find death.

Tode lachen (sich zu) *exp.* to laugh oneself silly • (lit); to laugh oneself to death.

Tode trinken/arbeiten (sich zu) *exp.* to drink/work oneself to death • (lit); [same].

Todesangst *exp.* scared to death • (lit); [same].

Todesstille *exp.* dead silence • (lit); [same].

Westentasche kennen (etwas wie seine) *exp.* to be very familiar with something (especially a location), to know something like the back of one's hand • (lit); to know something like one's vest pocket.

usage example: Was macht Hugo so in seiner Freizeit? Laß uns einfach mal sagen er kennt den Rotlichtbezirk **wie seine Westentasche**.

translation: What does Hugo do in his spare time? Let's just say he knows his way around the red light district.

literal translation: What does Hugo do in his spare time? Let's just say he knows the red light district like his vest pocket.

Practice The Vocabulary

(Answers to Lesson 1, p. 162)

A. Choose the correct word that completes the idiom.

1. Was ist dir nur für eine Laus über die (**Niere**, **Milz**, **Leber**) gelaufen?

2. Da liegt doch der (**Vogel**, **Hund**, **Fisch**) begraben.

3. Ich habe die Erdkundearbeit in den (**Sand**, **Dreck**, **Schlamm**) gesetzt.

4. Dabei dachte ich, ich kenne Europa wie meine (**Hemden**, **Hose**, **Westentasche**).

5. Erdkunde langweilt mich zu (**Tode**, **Leben**, **Schlaf**).

6. Frau Rater geht mir so auf die (**Zellen**, **Venen**, **Nerven**).

7. Warum spielst du die beleidigte (**Gurke**, **Leberwurst**, **Salami**)?

8. Wir sind schon so lange ein Herz und eine (**Seele**, **Leber**, **Lunge**).

B. CROSSWORD
Fill in the crossword puzzle on the opposite page by choosing the correct word(s) from the list below.

FASSUNG	**LEBERWURST**
HALS	**MISTSTÜCK**
HERZ	**NERVEN**
HUND	**SAND**
LEBER	**SCHNITZER**

Across

1. **_____ begraben (da liegt der)** *exp.* to be the root of one's problem • (lit); that's where the dog lies burried.

17. **einen groben _____ machen** *exp.* to make a big mistake, to blow it • (lit); to allow oneself a rough wood cut.

23. **_____ gehen (auf die)** *exp.* to annoy someone • (lit); to get on one's nerves.

29. **_____ bringen (aus der)** *exp.* to throw someone for a loop • (lit); to bring someone out of composure.

34. **_____** *exp.* (insult especially for a woman) dirtbag • (lit); piece of manure.

Down

1. **in den falschen _____ kriegen (etwas)** *exp.* to take something the wrong way • (lit); to get down the wrong throat.

15. **_____ spielen (die beleidigte)** *exp.* to get in a huff • (lit); to play the pouting Liverwurst.

16. **Laus über die _____ gelaufen (jemandem ist eine)** *exp.* said of someone who is being bugged by something • (lit); someone had a louse run over his liver.

18. **ein _____ und eine Seele sein** *exp.* to be inseparable • (lit); to be one heart and one soul.

35. **in den _____ setzen (etwas)** *exp.* to fail something miserably • (lit); to set something in the sand.

CROSSWORD PUZZLE

C. Match the columns.

☐ 1. What's bugging you?

☐ 2. I failed the geography test.

☐ 3. That's the root of your problem.

☐ 4. That really threw me for a loop.

☐ 5. Why are you so ticked off?

☐ 6. I can't believe that I could blow it like this.

☐ 7. He gets on my nerves.

☐ 8. We're great friends.

☐ 9. I hope you don't take this the wrong way.

☐ 10. I know Paris like the back of my hand.

A. **Ich habe die Erdkundearbeit in den Sand gesetzt.**

B. **Was ist dir nur für eine Laus über die Leber gelaufen?**

C. **Da liegt doch der Hund begraben.**

D. **Warum spielst du die beleidigte Leberwurst?**

E. **Ich hoffe, du kriegst das jetzt nicht in den falschen Hals.**

F. **Da habe ich mir wirklich einen groben Schnitzer erlaubt.**

G. **Das hat mich wirklich aus der Fassung gebracht.**

H. **Er geht mir so auf die Nerven.**

I. **Ich kenne Paris wie meine Westentasche.**

J. **Wir sind schon so lange ein Herz und eine Seele.**

D. DICTATION 🔲
Test Your Oral Comprehension

(This dictation can be found in Appendix A on page 174).

If you are following along with your cassette, you will now hear a series of sentences from the opening dialogue. These sentences will be read by a native speaker at normal conversational speed (which may seem fast to you at first). In addition, the words will be pronounced *as you would actually hear them in a conversation,* including many common reductions.

The first time the sentences are presented, simply listen in order to get accustomed to the speed and heavy use of reductions. The sentences will then be read again with a pause after each to give you time to write down what you heard. The third time the sentences are read, follow along with what you have written.

"ein Hühnchen mit jemandem zu rupfen haben"

(trans): *to have a bone to pick with someone*
(lit): *to have a chicken to pluck with someone*

Dialogue in slang

Auf der Party

Manuela: Ich kann gar nicht glauben, daß ich mich von dir **breitschlagen lassen** habe, zu deiner Büroparty mitzukommen. Ich fühle mich wie **das fünfte Rad am Wagen**, alle sind so **aufgetakelt**. Ach du meine Güte! Das ist ja **ein Bild für die Götter**! Wie kann eine ältere Frau nur etwas so freizügiges tragen?

Angela: Das ist Frau Meier. Sie ist fürchterlich. Mit ihr **habe ich auch noch ein Hühnchen zu rupfen**. Ich habe ihr etwas **unter vier Augen** anvertraut, und sie mußte es gleich im Büro **an die große Glocke hängen**! Na, aber jetzt **drehe ich den Spieß um**.

Manuela: Oh, bitte. Bloß nicht! Wenn du schon **reinen Tisch machen** mußt, tu es bitte zu einem anderen Zeitpunkt.

Angela: Von wegen! Der werde ich **die Leviten lesen**! Sie sieht aus, als ob sie **kein Wässerchen trüben könnte**, na, ihr **verpasse ich einen Denkzettel**!

Manuela: Warum gehst du jetzt zum Büffet? Heh! Was hast du mit der Sahnetorte vor?

Lesson Two

Translation of dialogue

Manuela: I can't believe I let you **talk me into** coming to your office party. I feel like **a third wheel**. Everyone's so **dressed up**! Wow! **Get a load of that!** How can an older woman wear something so revealing?

Angela: That's Ms. Meier. She's awful. I have a real **bone to pick with her**, too. I **told her something private**, and she **broadcasted** it to the entire office! Well, I'm going to **turn the tables** right now.

Manuela: Oh, please. Please don't! If you need **to clear the air**, do it privately.

Angela: No way! I'm going **to read her the riot act**! She looks so **innocent**. Well, I'm going **to teach her a lesson**.

Manuela: Why are you going to the buffet table? Hey! Where are you going with that cream pie?!

Lesson Two

At the Party

Manuela: I can't believe I let you **slap me wide** into coming to your office party. I feel like **the fifth wheel on a cart**. Everyone's so **all sails set**. Wow, my goodness! That's a **picture for the gods**! How can an older woman wear something so revealing?

Angela: That's Ms. Meier. She's awful. I **have a chicken to pluck** with her, too. I told her something **under four eyes**, and she had **to hang it from the big bell**! Well, I'm going **to turn the skewer around** right now.

Manuela: Oh, please. Please don't! If you need **to clear the table**, do it some other time.

Angela: No way! I'm going **to read to her from the book of Leviticus**! She looks like **she could cloud no small water**. Well, I'm going **to issue her a thinking note**.

Manuela: Why are you going to the buffet table? Hey! Where are you going with that cream pie?

Vocabulary

aufgetakelt sein *exp.* to get all dolled up • (lit); with all sails set.

usage example: Frau Schulze kam völlig **aufgetakelt** in die Kirche. Ihr Minirock und die hohen Schuhe waren wirklich unangemessen.

translation: Miss Schulze came to church all dolled up. Her miniskirt and those high heels were really inappropriate.

literal translation: Miss Schulze came to church with all sails set. Her miniskirt and those high heels were really inappropriate.

Augen sprechen (mit jemandem unter vier) *exp.* to speak privately with someone • (lit); to talk under four eyes.

usage example: Ich muß dir eine Geheimnis anvertrauen, können wir irgendwo **unter vier Augen sprechen**?

translation: I have to tell you a secret. Can we talk somewhere in private?

literal translation: I have to tell you a secret. Can we talk somewhere under four eyes?

OTHER IDIOMS USING "AUGE/AUGEN":

aller Augen (vor) *exp.* in front of everyone • (lit); before all eyes.

Auge behalten (etwas im) *exp.* to bear something in mind • (lit); to keep something in the eye.

Auge beleidigen (das) *exp.* to be an eyesore • (lit); to offend the eye.

Auge fassen (etwas ins) *exp.* to contemplate something • (lit); to seize something in the eye.

Auge geworfen haben (auf etwas ein) *exp.* to have one's sight set on something • (lit); to have thrown an eye on something.

Auge haben (etwas im) *exp.* to have one's eye on something • (lit); to have something in the eye.

Auge riskieren (ein) *exp.* to have a look • (lit); to risk an eye.

Auge stechen (ins) *exp.* to catch the eye • (lit); to stab in the eye.

Auge um Auge *exp.* an eye for an eye • (lit); eye for eye.

Auge zumachen (kein) *exp.* not to sleep a wink • (lit); not to close an eye.

Augen sehen (jemanden/etwas mit anderen) *exp.* to see someone/something in a different light • (lit); to see someone/something with different eyes.

Augen (in meinen) *exp.* in my opinion • (lit); in my eyes.

Augen an etwas weiden (die) *exp.* to feast one's eyes on • (lit); to graze the eyes on something.

Augen aus dem Kopf weinen (sich die) *exp.* to cry one's eyes out • (lit); to cry one's eyes out of the head.

Augen, aus dem Sinn (aus den) *exp.* out of sight, out of mind • (lit); out of the eyes, out of the mind.

Augen gesehen haben (etwas mit eigenen) *exp.* to have seen something with one's own eyes • (lit); [same]

Augen machen (große) *exp.* to be wide-eyed • (lit); to make big eyes.

Augen offen haben/offen halten (die) *exp.* to keep one's eyes peeled • (lit); to have/keep the eyes open.

Augen öffnen (jemandem die) *exp.* to open someone's eyes • (lit); [same].

Augen schließen (die) *exp.* to fall asleep • (lit); to close the eyes.

Augen sehen (jemandem in die) *exp.* to look someone in the eye(s) • (lit); to see someone in the eye.

Augen sind größer als der Magen/Bauch (die) *exp.* to have eyes bigger than one's stomach • (lit); the eyes are bigger than the stomach.

Augen vor etwas verschließen (die) *exp.* to close one's eyes to something • (lit); to close the eyes before something.

Augenblick *exp.* a moment, blink of an eye • (lit); [same].

Augenweide *exp.* pleasing to the eye • (lit); eye-grazing.

blauäugig *exp.* naive • (lit); blue-eyed.

blaues Auge (ein) *exp.* a black eye • (lit); a blue eye.

bloßen Auge (mit dem) *exp.* with the naked eye • (lit); with bare eyes.

da muß man seine Augen überall (hinten und vorn) haben *exp.* you need eyes in the back of your head • (lit); one must have one's eyes everywhere (or back and front).

geistigen Auge (vor meinem) *exp.* in my mind's eye • (lit); before my spiritual eye.

schöne Augen machen *exp.* to flirt with someone • (lit); to make pretty eyes.

schöne/verliebte Augen machen (jemandem) *exp.* to make eyes at someone (lit); to make beautiful/loving eyes at someone.

sein Ziel im Auge behalten *exp.* to keep one's goal in mind • (lit); to keep one's goal in the eye.

sicheres Auge für etwas haben (ein) *exp.* to have a good eye for something • (lit); to have a sure eye for something.

soweit das Augen reicht *exp.* as far as the eye can see • (lit); as far as the eye reaches.

Bild für die Götter sein (ein) *exp.* to be a sight to behold •
(lit); to be a picture for the gods.

usage example: Jochen hat den ganzen Nachmittag in der Schlammpfütze gespielt — **ein Bild für die Götter**!

translation: Jochen played in a mud puddle all afternoon. It was a sight to behold!

literal translation: Jochen played in a mud puddle all afternoon. A picture for the gods!

OTHER IDIOMS USING "BILD":

Bild machen (sich ein) *exp.* to get the picture • (lit); to make a picture for oneself.

Bild von einem Mann/einer Frau (ein) *exp.* a picture perfect man/woman • (lit); a picture of a man/woman.

Bilde sein über (im) *exp.* to be aware of something • (lit); to be in the picture.

Kopf oder Zahl *exp.* heads or tails • (lit); head or number.

breitschlagen lassen (sich) *exp.* to let oneself be talked into doing
something • (lit); to let oneself be pounded flat and wide.

usage example: Ich habe mich schon wieder zum Abwaschen **breitschlagen lassen**.

translation: I let myself be talked into doing the dishes again.

literal translation: I let myself be pounded flat and wide into doing the dishes again.

NOTE: The verb **breitschlagen** means "to pound something until it is flat and wide." (**breit** *adj.* wide • **schlagen** *exp.* to hit, pound, slap).

Denkzettel verpassen (jemandem einen) *exp.* to teach someone a lesson • (lit); to issue someone a thinking note.

> usage example: Mein kleiner Bruder hat schon wieder mein Auto geliehen ohne zu fragen. Diesmal werde ich ihm aber **einen Denkzettel verpassen**!

> translation: My little brother borrowed my car again without asking. This time I'm going to teach him a lesson!

> literal translation: My little brother borrowed my car again without asking. This time I'm going to issue him a thinking note!

Glocke hängen (etwas an die große) *exp.* to spread the news, to broadcast something • (lit); to hang something on a big bell.

> usage example: Du solltest doch nicht **an die große Glocke hängen**, daß ich schwanger bin. Ich habe es noch nicht einmal meinen Eltern erzählt!

> translation: You weren't supposed to broadcast it to everyone that I'm pregnant. I haven't even told my parents yet!

> literal translation: You weren't supposed to hang it on a big bell that I'm pregnant. I haven't even told my parents yet!

Hühnchen mit jemandem zu rupfen haben (ein) *exp.* to have a bone to pick with someone • (lit); to have a chicken to pluck with someone.

> usage example: Mit dir habe ich noch **ein Hühnchen zu rupfen**, Lise. Wie kommt der Brandfleck in das neue Kleid, das ich dir geborgt hatte?!

> translation: I still have a bone to pick with you, Lise. How did the burned spot get on the new dress I lent you?!

> literal translation: I still have a chicken to pluck with you, Lise. How did the burned spot get in the new dress I lent you?!

Leviten lesen (jemandem die) *exp.* to read someone the riot act • (lit); to read to someone from the book of Leviticus (biblical).

> usage example: Der Hund hat schon wieder auf den Teppich gepinkelt? Ihm **lese** ich jetzt aber kräftig **die Leviten**!

translation: The dog peed on the carpet again? I'm gonna read him the riot act now!

literal translation: The dog peed on the carpet again? I'm gonna read him the book of Leviticus now!

Rad am Wagen sein (das fünfte) *exp.* to feel like a third wheel

• (lit); to feel like the fifth wheel on a cart.

usage example: Warum hast du mir nicht gesagt, daß dein Freund mit uns zum Konzert kommt? Ich fühle mich wie **das fünfte Rad am Wagen**!

translation: Why didn't you tell me your boyfriend was going with us to the concert? I feel completely out of place!

literal translation: Why didn't you tell me your boyfriend was going with us to the concert? I feel just like the fifth wheel on a cart!

OTHER IDIOMS USING "RAD":

Rad abhaben (ein) *exp.* to have a screw loose • (lit); to have wheel off.

Räder kommen (unter die) *exp.* to go to the dogs • (lit); to come under the wheels.

OTHER IDIOMS USING "WAGEN":

Wagen fahren (jemandem an den) *exp.* to tread on someone's toes • (lit); to drive on one's wagon.

reinen Tisch machen *exp.* to clear the air • (lit); to clear the table.

usage example: Dein Schweigen kann ich nicht länger ertragen. Laß uns das Geschehene besprechen und **reinen Tisch machen**.

translation: I can't stand your silence any longer. Let's talk about what happened and clear the air.

literal translation: I can't stand your silence any longer. Let's talk about what happened and clear the table.

OTHER IDIOMS USING "TISCH":

Tisch bitten (jemanden zu) *exp.* to request someone to the table • (lit); [same].

Tisch ziehen (jemanden über den) *exp.* to take someone to the cleaners • (lit); to pull someone over the table.

Tisch fallen lassen (etwas unter den) *exp.* not to bring something up • (lit); to let something drop under the table.

Spieß umdrehen (den) *exp.* to turn the tables • (lit); to turn the skewer around.

usage example: Helmut hat mich beschuldigt, unnötig viel Wasser beim Duschen zu verbrauchen. Da hab ich **den Spieß** einfach umgedreht, und ihn an sein stundenlanges Autowaschen erinnert.

translation: Helmut accused me of wasting water while showering. So, I turned the tables and reminded him of his lengthy car washes.

literal translation: Helmut accused me of wasting water while showering. So, I turned the skewer around and reminded him of his lengthy car washes.

OTHER IDIOMS USING "SPIEß":

Spießer *exp.* bourgeois, stuck-up person • (lit); one who pierces.

Wässerchen trüben können (kein) *exp.* to look very innocent, to look like butter wouldn't melt in one's mouth • (lit); not to be able to cloud waters.

usage example: Fritz sieht aus, als ob er **kein Wässerchen trüben könnte**. Dabei haben seine Lehrer aber viel mit ihm zu schaffen.

translation: Fritz looks so innocent but his teachers have a lot of trouble with him.

literal translation: Fritz looks like he could cloud no waters, but his teachers have a lot of trouble with him.

Practice The Vocabulary

(Answers to Lesson 2, p. 163)

A. Choose the correct definition of the idiom.

1. **aufgetakelt sein:**
   - ☐ a. to get all dolled up
   - ☐ b. to speak privately with someone

2. **Augen sprechen (mit jemandem unter vier):**
   - ☐ a. to speak privately with someone
   - ☐ b. to spread the news

3. **Bild für die Götter sein (ein):**
   - ☐ a. to feel out of place
   - ☐ b. to be a sight to behold

4. **breitschlagen lassen (sich):**
   - ☐ a. to let oneself be talked into doing something
   - ☐ b. to get all dolled up

5. **Denkzettel verpassen (jemandem einen):**
   - ☐ a. to read someone the riot act
   - ☐ b. to teach someone a lesson

6. **Glocke hängen (etwas an die große):**
   - ☐ a. to have a bone to pick with someone
   - ☐ b. to broadcast something

7. **Hühnchen mit jemandem zu rupfen haben (ein):**
   - ☐ a. to broadcast something
   - ☐ b. to have a bone to pick with someone

8. **Leviten lesen (jemandem die):**
   - ☐ a. to read someone the riot act
   - ☐ b. to feel out of place

9. **Rad am Wagen sein (das fünfte):**
   ☐ a. to let oneself be talked into doing something
   ☐ b. to feel out of place

10. **reinen Tisch machen:**
    ☐ a. to clear the air
    ☐ b. to be a sight for sore eyes

11. **Spieß umdrehen (den):**
    ☐ a. to turn the tables
    ☐ b. to have a bone to pick with someone.

12. **Wässerchen trüben können (kein):**
    ☐ a. to read someone the riot act
    ☐ b. to look like butter wouldn't melt in one's mouth

B. Match the columns.

☐ 1. I can't believe I let you talk me into coming to your office party.

A. **Mit ihr habe ich noch ein Hühnchen zu rupfen.**

☐ 2. What a sight!

B. **Das ist ja ein Bild für die Götter!**

☐ 3. I feel like a third wheel.

C. **Jetzt drehe ich den Spieß um.**

☐ 4. I have a bone to pick with her.

D. **Ich fühle mich wie das fünfte Rad am Wagen.**

☐ 5. I'm going to turn the tables right now.

E. **Ich habe ihr was unter vier Augen anvertraut.**

☐ 6. I told her something privately.

F. **Ich kann gar nicht glauben, daß ich mich von dir breitschlagen lassen habe, mit zu deiner Büroparty zu kommen.**

C. STEP 1: Circle the corresponding letter of the word that best completes the idiom.

STEP 2: Find your answer in the FIND-A-WORD puzzle on the opposite page.

1. Ich fühle mich wie das _____ Rad am Wagen.
   a. **dritte**   b. **vierte**   c. **fünfte**

2. Das ist ja ein _____ für die Götter!
   a. **Bild**   b. **Photographie**   c. **Gemälde**

3. Mit ihr habe ich auch noch ein _____ zu rupfen.
   a. **Adler**   b. **Täubchen**   c. **Hühnchen**

4. Sie sieht aus, als könnte sie kein _____ trüben.
   a. **Wässerchen**   b. **Pfützchen**   c. **Lüftchen**

5. Jetzt drehe ich den _____ um.
   a. **Speer**   b. **Harpune**   c. **Spieß**

6. Ich habe ihr was unter vier _____ zu sagen.
   a. **Ohren**   b. **Augen**   c. **Füßen**

7. Sie hat es gleich im Büro an die große _____ gehängt!
   a. **Glocke**   b. **Bimmel**   c. **Sirene**

8. Wenn du schon reinen _____ machen mußt, tue es bitte wo anders!
   a. **Stuhl**   b. **Fußboden**   c. **Tisch**

FIND-A-WORD PUZZLE

```
A Ü N Ü O A E A T J W E T
F P F S I B R Ä O A Ä S A
Ü A J P S D S U M D S T N
N R O I C E M N A O S C N
F S B E N K T C N T E E A
T S I S G B I L D E R Q U
E I R S I A A A H S C U G
X Y E A F L C N E C H E E
B G L O C K E D P A E J N
A V A A K A A R H R N E K
L Ü L H Ü H N C H E N T E
I A Y O T E O Ö K E U A W
S T I S C H Ä L N S T I Ü
```

D. DICTATION 📼
Test Your Oral Comprehension

(This dictation can be found in Appendix A on page 174).

If you are following along with your cassette, you will now hear a series of sentences from the opening dialogue. These sentences will be read by a native speaker at normal conversational speed (which may seem fast to you at first). In addition, the words will be pronounced *as you would actually hear them in a conversation,* including many common reductions.

The first time the sentences are presented, simply listen in order to get accustomed to the speed and heavy use of reductions. The sentences will then be read again with a pause after each to give you time to write down what you heard. The third time the sentences are read, follow along with what you have written.

LEKTION DREI

"jemanden auf den Arm nehmen"

(trans): to pull someone's leg
(lit): to take someone up on one's arm

Dialogue in slang

Der Hausgast

Dirk: Wie geht es so mit eurem neuen Hausgast?

Andrea: Ach, ich könnte **mich grün und blau ärgern**, daß ich eingewilligt habe, Manfreds Bruder hier wohnen zu lassen bis er eine Wohnung gefunden hat. Er ist ein **Schmuddel wie er im Buche steht**. Ich **habe so die Nase von ihm voll**. Unser Haus war immer **wie aus dem Ei gepellt**. Schau es dir jetzt mal an!

Dirk: Ich habe dich noch nie so aufgeregt gesehen. Du scheinst ja wirklich **mit deinem Latein am Ende** zu sein. Ich bin ja richtig froh, daß ich **nicht in deiner Haut stecke**. Was gedenkst du zu unternehmen?

Andrea: Ich weiß nicht. Wir haben schon **ein Auge zugedrückt**, als er unser Telefon für Ferngespräche benutzte. Ich habe nicht mal was gesagt, als er meine wertvolle Vase zerbrach. Aber heute hat er den Braten **verputzt**, den ich zum Abendessen servieren wollte.

Dirk: **Du nimmst mich doch auf den Arm**!

Andrea: Nein, überhaupt nicht. Ich gebe ihm schon immer **einen Wink mit dem Zaunpfahl**, damit er endlich geht, aber er **schnallt es** einfach nicht.

Dirk: Ich glaube, du mußt aufhören, **um den heißen Brei zu reden** und ihm einfach sagen, daß er sich **zum Teufel scheren soll**.

Andrea: Ich habe eine bessere Idee. Er kann bleiben. Ich gehe!

Lesson Three

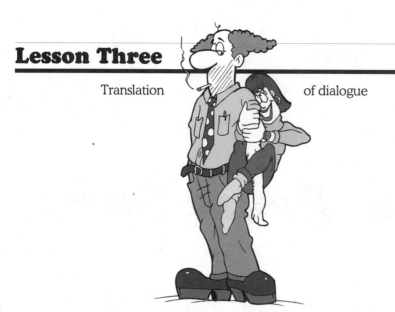

Translation of dialogue

Dirk: How's everything going with your new house guest?

Andrea: I'm so **mad at myself** for agreeing to let Manfred's brother stay here until he finds an apartment. He's a **textbook** example of a **messy person**. I'm totally **fed up** with him. Our house used to be **immaculate**. Now look at it!

Dirk: I've never seen you so upset. You look like you're **at your wits end**. I'm glad I'm not **in your shoes**. What are you going to do about it?

Andrea: I don't know. We **looked the other way** when he used the phone for long distance calls. I didn't say anything when he broke my precious vase. But today he **ate** the roast I was planning on serving for dinner!

Dirk: **You're pulling my leg**.

Andrea: Not at all. I keep **dropping hints** for him to leave, but he just **doesn't get it**!

Dirk: I think you need **to stop beating around the bush** and just **tell him to get lost**.

Andrea: I've got a better idea. He can stay. I'll leave.

Literal translation of dialogue

The House Guest

Dirk: How's everything going with your new house guest?

Andrea: I could **anger myself green and blue** for agreeing to let Manfred's brother stay here until he finds an apartment. He's a **messy person** as **described in a book**. I **got the nose full of him**. Our house used to look **like peeled from an egg**. Now, look at it!

Dirk: I've never seen you so upset. You look like you're at the **end with your Latin**. I'm glad I'm not **stuck in your skin**. What are you going to do about it?

Andrea: I don't know. We **squeezed an eye shut** when he used the phone for long distance calls. I didn't say anything when he broke my precious vase. But today, he **polished off** the roast I was planning on serving for dinner.

Dirk: **You're taking me up the arm**!

Andrea: Not at all. I keep giving him a **hint with the fencepost** to leave, but he just **doesn't get it**!

Dirk: I think you need to stop **talking around the hot porridge** and just **tell him to go to the devil**.

Andrea: I've got a better idea. He can stay. I'll leave.

Vocabulary

Arm nehmen (jemanden auf den) *exp.* to pull one's leg • (lit); to take someone up on one's arm.

> usage example: Andrea geht dieses das Wochenende zelten? Du willst mich wohl **auf den Arm nehmen**. Sie hat doch Platzangst. Sie schläft doch niemals in einem Zelt!
>
> translation: Andrea is going camping this weekend? You're pulling my leg. She's claustrophobic. She'll never sleep in a tent!
>
> literal translation: Andrea is going camping this weekend? You want to take me up the arm. She's claustrophobic. She'll never sleep in a tent!
>
> OTHER IDIOMS USING "ARM":
>
>> **Arm in Arm gehen** *exp.* to walk arm in arm • (lit); to go arm in arm.
>>
>> **Arme greifen (jemandem unter die)** *exp.* to give someone a hand financially • (lit); to grab someone under the arms.
>>
>> **Arme laufen (jemandem in die)** *exp.* to meet someone by chance • (lit); to walk into someone's arms.
>>
>> **offenen Armen empfangen (jemanden mit)** *exp.* to receive someone with open arms • (lit); [same].

Auge zudrücken (ein) *exp.* to turn a blind eye • (lit); to squeeze one eye shut.

> usage example: Der Verkehrspolizist hat nochmal **ein Auge zugedrückt** und mir keinen Strafzettel gegeben.
>
> translation: The cop turned a blind eye and didn't give me a ticket.
>
> literal translation: The cop squeezed one eye shut and didn't give me a ticket.

OTHER IDIOMS USING "AUGE":

SEE: page 21.

Buche steht (wie er/sie/es im) *exp.* to be a textbook example of
something • (lit); to be depicted in a book.

usage example: Marion ist eine Verkäuferin **wie sie im Buche steht**. Sie hat diese Woche dreimal mehr verkauft als ihre Mitarbeiterinnen.

translation: Marion is a textbook example of a salesperson. She sold three times as much this week as her co-workers.

literal translation: Marion is a salesperson as depicted in a book. She sold three times as much this week as her co-workers.

OTHER IDIOMS USING "BUCH/BUCHE":

Buchführung *exp.* to keep books (accounting) • (lit); to lead a book.

Büchern sitzen (über den) *exp.* to pore over one's books • (lit); to sit over the books.

wie ein Buch mit sieben Siegeln *exp.* incomprehensible • (lit); like a book with seven seals.

wie ein Buch reden *exp.* to talk like a book • (lit); [same].

Ei gepellt (wie aus dem) *exp.* to be as neat as a pin • (lit); like peeled
from an egg.

usage example: Alle Schüler sahen auf der Abschlußfeier **wie aus dem Ei gepellt** aus, bis auf Hugo, der in Jeans und T-shirt kam.

translation: All the students looked immaculate at their graduation ceremony except for Hugo, who came in jeans and T-shirt.

literal translation: All the student looked peeled from an egg at their graduation ceremony except for Hugo, who came in jeans and T-shirt.

OTHER IDIOMS USING "Ei":

das Ei des Kolumbus *exp.* (said of something extremely simple yet not obvious) to be under one's nose the whole time • (lit); the egg of Columbus.

das sind ungelegte Eier! *exp.* We'll cross that bridge when we come to it! • (lit); these are unlaid eggs.

wie ein Ei dem andern gleichen *exp.* to be as alike as two peas in a pod • (lit); to be like one egg to the other.

wie ein rohes Ei behandeln (jemanden) *exp.* to handle someone with kid gloves • (lit); to treat someone like a raw egg.

grün und blau ärgern (sich) *exp.* to be furious, to see red • (lit); to anger oneself green and blue.

usage example: Ich **ärgere mich grün und blau**, daß ich diese Woche kein Lotto gespielt habe. Alle meine Zahlen wurden gezogen!

translation: I'm so furious that I didn't play the lottery this week. All my numbers were drawn!

literal translation: I anger myself green and blue that I didn't play the lottery this week. All my numbers were drawn!

OTHER IDIOMS USING "GRÜN":

grün und blau schlagen (jemanden) *exp.* to beat someone black and blue • (lit); to beat someone green and blue.

Grüne fahren (ins) *exp.* to drive to the country • (lit); to drive into the green.

Grüner (ein) *n.* • **1.** an ecologist, environmentalist • **2.** mucus in one's throat, "loogie" (lit); a green.

Grünes Licht (für etwas) geben/haben *exp.* to give/have the green light to do something • (lit); to give/have a green light (for something).

nicht grün sein (jemandem) *exp.* to have it in for someone • (lit); not to be green to someone.

noch grün hinter den Ohren sein *exp.* inexperienced, wet behind the ears • (lit); to be still green behind the ears.

OTHER IDIOMS USING "BLAU":

blau machen *exp.* to take a day off • (lit); to make blue.

blau sein *exp.* to be drunk, plastered • (lit); to be blue.

blauen Auge davonkommen (mit einem) *exp.* to get off unscathed • (lit); to get away with a blue eye.

blaues Auge (ein) *exp.* a black eye • (lit); a blue eye.

Haut stecken wollen (nicht in jemandes) *exp.* not to want to be in someone's shoes • (lit); not to want to be stuck in someone's skin.

usage example: Ich möchte wirklich **nicht in deiner Haut stecken**, wenn Mutti herausfindet, daß du ihr Auto geschrottet hast.

translation: I really wouldn't want to be in your shoes when Mom finds out you wrecked her car.

literal translation: I really wouldn't want to be stuck in your skin when mom finds out that you wrecked her car.

OTHER IDIOMS USING "HAUT":

auf der faulen Haut liegen / sich auf die faule Haut legen *exp.* not to lift a finger • (lit); to lie on the lazy skin / to lie down on one's lazy skin.

dicke Haut haben (eine) *exp.* to be thick-skinned • (lit); to have a thick skin.

ehrliche Haut (eine) *exp.* an honest person • (lit); an honest skin.

Haut durchnäßt (bis auf die) *exp.* soaked to the skin • (lit); wet down to the skin.

Haut fahren (aus der) *exp.* to jump out of one's skin • (lit); to drive out of one's skin.

Haut gehen (jemandem unter die) *exp.* to get under someone's skin • (lit); [same].

Haut retten (seine eigene) *exp.* to save one's own skin • (lit); [same].

Haut und Haar (mit) *exp.* completely, entirely • (lit); with skin and hair.

Haut und Knochen sein (nur) *exp.* to be nothing but skin and bones • (lit); to be only skin and bones.

heißen Brei reden (um den) *exp.* to beat around the bush • (lit); to talk around the hot porridge.

usage example: Sag mir einfach was du willst! Hör auf, **um den heißen Brei zu reden**!

translation: Just tell me what you want! Stop beating around the bush!

literal translation: Just tell me what you want! Stop talking around the hot porridge!

OTHER IDIOMS USING "BREI":

zu Brei schlagen (jemanden) *exp.* to beat someone to a pulp • (lit); [same].

Latein am Ende sein (mit seinem) *exp.* to be at one's wits' end • (lit); to be at the end with one's Latin.

usage example: Dreimal habe ich versucht, Hilde ins Gewissen zu reden, aber sie besteht darauf, eine Tätowierung machen zu lassen. Nun **bin ich mit meinem Latein am Ende**!

translation: I tried three times to talk some sense into Hilde. She still insists on getting a tatoo. I'm at my wits' end!

literal translation: I tried three times to talk some sense into Hilde. She still insists on getting a tatoo. Now I'm at the end with my Latin!

Nase von etwas/jemandem voll haben (die) *exp.* to be fed up, to have had all one can tolerate • (lit); to have the nose full of something or someone.

usage example: Wanda hat ihren Freund zum zweiten Mal beim fremdgehen erwischt. Nun hat sie endgültig **die Nase von ihm voll**!

translation: Wanda caught her boyfriend cheating on her for the second time. Now she's completely had it with him!

literal translation: Wanda caught her boyfriend cheating on her for the second time. Now she's had the nose full of him!

OTHER IDIOMS USING "NASE":

es liegt vor deiner Nase *exp.* it's right under your nose • (lit); it lies before your nose.

feine Nase haben (eine) *exp.* to have a flair for something • (lit); to have a fine nose.

lange Nase machen (jemandem eine) *exp.* to thumb one's nose at someone • (lit); to make someone a long nose.

Nase binden (jemandem etwas auf die) *exp.* to get something off one's chest • (lit); to tie something on someone's nose.

Nase hochtragen (die) *exp.* to have one's nose in the air, to be conceited • (lit); to carry the nose high.

Nase in alles stecken (seine) *exp.* to poke one's nose into someone else's business • (lit); to put one's nose into everything.

Nase liegen (auf der) *exp.* to be laid up (sick) • (lit); to lie on the nose.

Nase reiben (jemandem etwas unter die) *exp.* to rub someone's nose in something • (lit); to rub something under someone's nose.

Nase vorn haben (die) *exp.* to be a step ahead, to be in the know • (lit); to have the nose in front.

Naseweis *n.* a nosey person • (lit); nose-know.

Tür vor der Nase zuwerfen (jemandem die) *exp.* to slam the door in someone's face • (lit); to slam the door in front of the nose.

Schmuddel *n.* a messy person • (lit); see note below.

usage example: Günter war schon immer ein **Schmuddel**. Jetzt hat er sich endlich entschlossen, sein Talent zu nutzen, und Pennbruder zu werden.

translation: Günter always was a filthy person. Now he has finally decided to make use of his talent and become a bum.

NOTE: This comes from the word **schmutz** meaning "dirt."

schnallen (etwas nicht) *exp.* not to understand something, not to catch on • (lit); not to buckle something.

usage example: Unsere Lehrerin hat uns die Matheaufgabe noch einmal erklärt, aber Eva hat sie immer noch **nicht geschnallt**.

translation: Our teacher explained the math problem again, but Eva still didn't get it.

literal translation: Our teacher explained the math problem again, but Eva still has not buckled it.

Teufel scheren (zum) *exp.* to get lost • (lit); to go to the devil.

usage example: Nachdem Schröder mehrere Male betrunken am Arbeitsplatz erschienen ist, sagte ihm der Vorarbeiter ihm, er solle sich **zum Teufel scheren**.

translation: After showing up drunk at work several times, Schröder's supervisor told him to get lost.

literal translation: After showing up drunk at work several times, Schröder's supervisor told him to go to the devil.

verputzen (etwas) *exp.* to devour something • (lit); to polish off something.

> usage example: Olaf hat den ganzen Truthahn allein **verputzt**. Wo steckt er das nur hin?
>
> translation: Olaf ate the whole turkey by himself. Where does he put it?
>
> literal translation: Olaf polished off the whole turkey by himself. Where does he put it?

OTHER IDIOMS USING "VERPUTZEN":

> **verputzen können (jemanden nicht)** *exp.* to be unable to stand someone • (lit); not to be able to digest someone.

Wink mit dem Zaunpfahl (ein) *exp.* a broad hint • (lit); a hint with the fencepost.

> usage example: Ich glaube das sollte **ein Wink mit dem Zaunpfahl** sein, als Elli sagte, sie sei in das Kleid im Schaufenster verliebt.
>
> translation: I think Elli was dropping a broad hint when she said she was in love with the dress in the window.
>
> literal translation: I think it was supposed to be a hint with the fencepost when Elli said she was in love with the dress in the window.

Practice The Vocabulary

(Answers to Lesson 3, p. 164)

A. Choose the correct word that completes the idiom.

1. Ich könnte mich grün und (**rot**, **blau**, **orange**) ärgern, daß ich eingewilligt habe, Manfreds Bruder hier wohnen zu lassen bis er eine Wohnung gefunden hat.

2. Ich glaube, du mußt aufhören, um den (**heißen**, **warmen**, **kalten**) Brei zu reden.

3. Wir haben schon ein (**Ohr**, **Herz**, **Auge**) zugedrückt, als er unser Telefon für Ferngespräche benützte.

4. Du nimmst mich doch auf den (**Kopf**, **Arm**, **Rücken**)!

5. Ich habe so die (**Ohren**, **Hände**, **Nase**) von ihm voll.

6. Unser Haus war immer wie aus dem (**Apfel**, **Ei**, **Fisch**) gepellt.

7. Ich bin ja richtig froh, daß ich nicht in deiner (**Hose**, **Fell**, **Haut**) stecke.

8. Du mußt ihm einfach sagen, daß er sich zum (**Teufel**, **Engel**, **Geist**) scheren soll.

B. Match the columns.

☐ 1. I'm so mad at myself.

☐ 2. I think you need to stop beating around the bush.

☐ 3. He's a textbook example of a messy person.

☐ 4. We looked the other way when he used the phone for long distance calls.

☐ 5. I'm totally fed up with him.

☐ 6. You're pulling my leg!

☐ 7. I'm glad I'm not in your shoes.

☐ 8. You look like you're at your wits' end.

☐ 9. Our house used to be immaculate.

A. **Du nimmst mich doch auf den Arm!**

B. **Ich glaube, du mußt aufhören, um den heißen Brei zu reden.**

C. **Wir haben schon ein Auge zugedrückt, als er unser Telefon für Ferngespräche benutzt hat.**

D. **Ich habe so die Nase von ihm voll.**

E. **Ich bin ja richtig froh, daß ich nicht in deiner Haut stecke.**

F. **Du scheinst ja wirklich mit deinem Latein am Ende zu sein.**

G. **Ich könnte mich grün und blau ärgern.**

H. **Unser Haus war immer wie aus dem Ei gepellt.**

I. **Er ist ein Schmuddel, wie er im Buche steht.**

C. Choose the definition that goes with the idiom.

A. a broad hint

B. a messy person

C. not to want to be in someone's shoes

D. not to understand something

E. to beat around the bush

F. to devour something

G. to get lost

H. to be a textbook example of something

I. to be extremely upset

J. to be fed up

K. to be at one's wits' end

L. to be immaculate

M. to turn a blind eye

N. to pull someone's leg

☐ 1. **Nase von etwas voll haben (die)** *exp.*

☐ 2. **Arm nehmen (jemanden auf den)** *exp.*

☐ 3. **Buche steht (wie er/sie/es im)** *exp.*

☐ 4. **schnallen (etwas nicht)** *exp.*

☐ 5. **Schmuddel** *exp.*

☐ 6. **Wink mit dem Zaunpfahl (ein)** *exp.*

☐ 7. **Ei gepellt (wie aus dem)** *exp.*

☐ 8. **verputzen (etwas)** *exp.*

☐ 9. **heißen Brei zu reden (um den)** *exp.*

☐ 10. **Teufel scheren (zum)** *exp.*

☐ 11. **Auge zudrücken (ein)** *exp.*

☐ 12. **Haut stecken wollen (nicht in jemandens)** *exp.*

☐ 13. **Latein am Ende sein (mit seinem)** *exp.*

☐ 14. **grün und blau ärgern (sich)** *exp.*

D. DICTATION
Test Your Oral Comprehension

(This dictation can be found in Appendix A on page 174).

If you are following along with your cassette, you will now hear a series of sentences from the opening dialogue. These sentences will be read by a native speaker at normal conversational speed (which may seem fast to you at first). In addition, the words will be pronounced *as you would actually hear them in a conversation*, including many common reductions.

The first time the sentences are presented, simply listen in order to get accustomed to the speed and heavy use of reductions. The sentences will then be read again with a pause after each to give you time to write down what you heard. The third time the sentences are read, follow along with what you have written.

"den Nagel auf den Kopf treffen"

(lit): to hit the nail on the head

Dialogue in slang

Im Restaurant

Thomas: Entschuldige, daß ich so spät bin, aber ich **hatte heute soviel um die Ohren** bei der Arbeit.

Maria: Kein Problem. Ich war auch zu spät. Ich hatte wieder eine Auseinandersetzung mit meiner Chefin.

Thomas: Sie scheint ja ständig **einen Streit vom Zaun zu brechen**. Du mußt wirklich lernen, nicht jedes ihrer **Worte auf die Goldwaage zu legen**.

Maria: Ich weiß. Ich muß ihr wirklich **ein Dorn im Auge sein**. Sie hat mich die ganze Woche lang ohne Grund **links liegen lassen**, dabei ist sie doch sonst **nicht auf den Mund gefallen**. Ich verstehe das nicht.

Thomas: Vielleicht ist sie eifersüchtig, weil du bei allen anderen **einen Stein im Brett hast** und sie nicht.

Maria: Ich glaube, da hast du **den Nagel auf den Kopf getroffen**. Na ja, **ich lasse mir darüber keine grauen Haare wachsen**. Ich habe gerade herausgefunden, daß ich ab Montag ihren Chef ersetzen werde. Wenn sie sich dann **im Ton vergreift**, werde ich ihr gehörig **den Marsch blasen**!

Lesson Four

Thomas: Sorry I'm late, but I got **so busy** at work today.

Maria: No problem. I was late, too. I just had another argument with my boss.

Thomas: She always seems to **pick fights** with you. You really need to learn to take what she says **with a grain of salt**.

Maria: I know. I must be a real **thorn in her side**. She **gave me the cold shoulder** all week for no reason. With everyone else in the office, she's rather **outspoken**. I don't understand it.

Thomas: Maybe she's jealous because you're **in good graces** with everyone and she's not.

Maria: I think you've **hit the nail on the head**. Well, I'm not going to **lose any sleep over it**. I just found out that starting Monday, I'm going to replace her boss. Then if she **puts me down** at all, I'll **give it to her**!

Lesson Four

Im Restaurant

Thomas: Sorry, I'm late. I had so much **around the ears** at work today.

Maria: No problem. I was late, too. I just had another argument with my boss.

Thomas: She always seems **to break an argument off the fence**. You really need to learn not to put each of her **words on the jeweler's scale**.

Maria: I know. I must be a real **thorn in her eyes** . She **let me lie left** all week for no reason, even **though she is usually not like she fell on her mouth**. I don't understand it.

Thomas: Maybe she's just jealous because you've **got a stone in the board** with everyone and she doesn't.

Maria: I think you **hit the nail on the head**. Well, I'm not **going to grow grey hairs over it**. I just found out that starting Monday, I'm going to replace her boss. Then if she **hits the wrong chord**, I'm going **to blow her the march**!

Vocabulary

Dorn im Auge sein (jemandem ein) *exp.* to be a thorn in one's side • (lit); to be a thorn in someone's eye.

    usage example: Ich bin froh, daß wir endlich unser Haus streichen. Die alte Farbe war mir schon immer **ein Dorn im Auge**.

    translation: I'm glad we're finally painting our house. The old color has always been a thorn in my side.

    literal translation: I'm glad we're finally painting our house. The old color has always been a thorn in my eye.

Keine grauen Haare wachsen lassen (sich) *exp.* not to lose sleep over something • (lit); not to grow grey hair over something.

    usage example: Man sagt, daß wir eines Tages ein großes Erdbeben haben werden, aber darüber lasse ich mir **keine grauen Haare wachsen**. Wenn es passiert, passiert es eben.

    translation: They say that we're going to have a large earthquake some day, but I'm not going to lose any sleep over it. If it happens, it happens.

    literal translation: They say that we're going to have a large earthquake some day, but I'm not going to grow any grey hair over it. If it happens, it happens.

OTHER IDIOMS USING "HAAR":

    Haar gleichen (jemandem aufs) *exp.* to be the spitting image of someone • (lit); to be like someone to the hair.

    Haar in der Suppe finden (ein) *exp.* to knitpick, to find fault with something/someone, to find a fly in the ointment • (lit); to find a hair in the soup.

Haare auf den Zähnen haben *exp.* to be a tough customer • (lit); to have hairs on the teeth.

Haare ausraufen (sich die) *exp.* to tear one's hair out • (lit); [same].

Haare lassen müssen *exp.* **1.** to suffer heavy losses • **2.** to get ripped off • (lit); to have to leave hairs.

Haaren herbeigezogen (an den) *exp.* to be far-fetched • (lit); to be dragged by the hairs.

Haaren liegen (sich in den) *exp.* to be in disagreement • (lit); to lie in one's hairs.

haargenau *adj.* exactly, to a T • (lit); hair exact.

kein gutes Haar an jemandem lassen *exp.* to rip a person to pieces (through criticism) • (lit); not to let a good hair on someone.

links liegen lassen (etwas) *exp.* to pass something up • (lit); to leave something to the left.

    usage example: Schwalli kann einfach nichts Süßes **links liegen lassen**, deshalb ist er so dick.

    translation: Schwalli can't pass up sweets. That's why he's so big.

    literal translation: Schwalli can't leave sweets lying to the left. That's why he's so big.

    ALSO: **links liegen lassen (jemanden)** *exp.* to give someone the cold shoulder.

Marsch blasen (jemandem den) *exp.* to reprimand someone • (lit); to blow someone the march.

    usage example: Jetzt reichts! Schulze hat mir schon wieder die Einfahrt zugeparkt. Dem werde ich **den Marsch blasen**!

    translation: That does it! Schulze blocked my driveway again. I'm gonna let him have it!

    literal translation: That does it! Schulze blocked my driveway again. I'm gonna blow him the march!

Mund gefallen sein (nicht auf den) *exp.* not to be at a loss for words • (lit); not to be fallen on one's mouth.

usage example: Ursula ist nicht gerade **auf den Mund gefallen**. Während der Versammlung wußte sie stets, was sie zu sagen hatte.

translation: Ursula is never at a loss for words. During the meeting, she always knew what to say.

literal translation: Ursula never fell on her mouth. During the meeting, she always knew what to say.

OTHER IDIOMS USING "MUND":

in aller Munde (sein) *exp.* everyone's talking about... • (lit); to be in everyone's mouth.

Mund halten (den) *exp.* to shut up • (lit); to hold the mouth.

Mund über etwas halten (seinen) *exp.* to keep something secret • (lit); to keep one's mouth shut about something.

Mund reden (jemandem nach dem) *exp.* to butter someone up • (lit); to talk after someone's mouth.

Mund verbrennen (sich den) *exp.* to put one's foot in one's mouth • (lit); to burn one's mouth.

Mund verziehen (seinen/den) *exp.* to make a face • (lit); to warp one's/the mouth.

Mund wäßrig machen (jemandem den) *exp.* to make someone's mouth water • (lit); [same].

Munde riechen (aus dem) *exp.* to have bad breath • (lit); to smell from the mouth.

mundfaul sein *adj.* not to be talkative • (lit); to be mouth lazy.

mundgerecht *adj.* bite-size • (lit); mouth just (or: just made for the mouth).

Nagel auf den Kopf treffen (den) *exp.* to be absolutely correct
• (lit); to hit the nail on the head.

usage example: Ich glaube, du hast **den Nagel auf den Kopf getroffen** als du sagtest, der Film sei völlig idiotisch.

translation: I think you had it exactly right when you said the film was totally idiotic.

literal translation: I think you hit the nail on the head when you said the film was totally idiotic.

OTHER IDIOMS USING "NAGEL":

> **Nagel hängen (etwas an den)** *exp.* to give something up • (lit); to hang something on the nail.
>
> **nigelnagelneu** *exp.* brand-new • (lit); nail-new.

OTHER IDIOMS USING "KOPF":

> **Dickkopf** *n.* a stubborn person • (lit); thick head.
>
> **Dummkopf** *n.* moron • (lit); dumb head.
>
> **durch den Kopf gehen lassen (sich etwas)** *exp.* to think something over • (lit); to let something go through one's head.
>
> **es geht um Kopf und Kragen** *exp.* it's a matter of life and death • (lit); it goes for head and neck.
>
> **Kopf an Kopf** *exp.* neck and neck • (lit); head to head.
>
> **Kopf einrennen (sich den)** *exp.* to beat one's head against a wall • (lit); to run one's head into something.
>
> **Kopf hinhalten [müssen] (den)** *exp.* to have to face the music • (lit); to have to offer one's head.
>
> **Kopf oben behalten (den)** *exp.* to keep up one's spirits • (lit); to keep the head up.
>
> **Kopf stellen (etwas auf den)** *exp.* to turn something upside-down • (lit); to put something on the head.
>
> **Kopf waschen (jemandem den)** *exp.* to tell someone off • (lit); to wash someone's head.

Kopf zu sagen (jemandem etwas auf den) *exp.* to tell someone something directly • (lit); to tell someone something to the head.

Kopflastig *n.* intellectual • (lit); head heavy.

nicht auf den Kopf spucken lassen (sich) *exp.* not to let people walk all over oneself • (lit); not to let oneself be spit on the head.

schweren Kopf haben *exp.* **1.** to have a hangover • **2.** to have a headache • (lit); to have a heavy head.

Stein im Brett haben (bei jemandem einen) *exp.* to be

in one's good graces • (lit); to have a stone in the board with someone.

usage example: Mein Vater hat bei meiner Oma einen **Stein im Brett**, weil er ihr immer im Garten hilft.

translation: My father is in good graces with my grandma because he always helps her with her garden.

literal translation: My father has a stone in the board with my grandma because he always helps her with her garden.

OTHER IDIOMS USING "STEIN":

ersten Stein werfen (den) *exp.* to cast the first stone • (lit); [same].

man soll nicht mit Steinen werfen, wenn man selbst in Glashaus sitzt *exp.* people who sit in glass houses shouldn't throw stones • (lit); one should not throw stones when one sits by oneself in a glass house.

Stein des Anstoßes *exp.* a stumbling-block • (lit); the stone of initiative.

Stein ins Rollen bringen (den) *exp.* to get the ball rolling • (lit); to get the stone rolling.

Streit vom Zaun brechen (einen) *exp.* to start an argument •
(lit); to break an argument off the fence.

> usage example: Irene braucht keinen Grund um **einen Streit vom**
> **Zaun zu brechen**. Ich glaube, sie zankt sich einfach
> gern.
>
> translation: Irene doesn't need a reason to start an argument. I think
> she really loves to fight.
>
> literal translation: Irene doesn't need a reason to break an argument off
> the fence. I think she really loves to fight.

> OTHER IDIOMS USING "STREIT":
> _____
>
> **Streit liegen (mit jemandem in)** *exp.* to be at
> odds with someone • (lit); to lie in argument with
> someone.
>
> **Streithahn** *n.* one who argues a lot • (lit);
> argument rooster.

Ton vergreifen (sich im) *exp.* to blow it • (lit); to hit the wrong
note.

> usage example: Hubert hat sich wirklich **im Ton vergriffen**, als er
> seinen Boss einen Idioten nannte.
>
> translation: Hubert really blew it when he called his boss an idiot.
>
> literal translation: Hubert really grabbed the wrong note when he called
> his boss an idiot.

> OTHER IDIOMS USING "TON":
> _____
>
> **gehört zum guten Ton (etwas)** *exp.* to be
> according to protocol • (lit); something belonging
> to the good tone.
>
> **in höchsten Tönen von jemandem/etwas**
> **reden** *exp.* to speak highly about someone/
> something • (lit); to speak in highest tones about
> someone/something.
>
> **Ton angeben (den)** *exp.* to set the tone (in a
> conversation) • (lit); [same].

viel um die Ohren haben *exp.* to be very busy, to be up to one's ears in work • (lit); to have much around the ears.

    usage example: Das Telefon klingelt pausenlos! Ich **habe zuviel um die Ohren**!

    translation: The phone's been ringing endlessly! I'm too busy!

    literal translation: The phone's been ringing endlessly! I have too much around the ears!

Wort auf die Goldwaage legen (nicht jedes) *exp.* to hang on one's every word • (lit); to put every word on the gold (jeweler's) scale.

    usage example: In einem Scheidungsfall wird **jedes Wort auf die Goldwaage gelegt**.

    translation: In a divorce case, they'll hang on every word.

    literal translation: In a divorce case, every single word will be put on the gold (jeweler's) scale.

OTHER IDIOMS USING "WORT":

    anderen Worten (mit) *exp.* in other words • (lit); with other words.

    beim Wort nehmen *exp.* to take someone up on one's offer • (lit); to take at the word.

    gutes Wort einlegen (für jemanden ein) *exp.* to put in a good word for someone • (lit); [same].

    keinem Wort erwähnen (etwas mit) *exp.* not to say a word about something • (lit); to mention something without words.

    nicht zu Wort kommen *exp.* not to get a word in edgewise • (lit); not to get to the word.

    ohne viele Worte zu machen *exp.* without further ado • (lit); without making many words.

    paar Worte sprechen (ein) *exp.* to make a toast • (lit); to speak a few words.

    sein Wort brechen *exp.* to break one's word • (lit); [same].

"Spar dir deine Worte!" *exp.* "Don't waste your breath!" • (lit); Save your words!

Wort aus dem Munde nehmen (jemandem das) *exp.* to take the words out of someone's mouth • (lit); [same].

Wort fallen (jemandem ins) *exp.* to cut someone short • (lit); to fall into someone's word.

Wort haben (das) *exp.* to have the floor • (lit); to have the word.

Wort halten *exp.* to keep one's word • (lit); [same].

Wort im Mund umdrehen (jemandem das) *exp.* to twist someone's words • (lit); to twist the word in someone's mouth.

Practice The Vocabulary

(Answers to Lesson 4, p. 164)

A. CROSSWORD
Fill in the crossword puzzle on the opposite page by choosing the correct word from the list below.

AUGE	MARSCH	STEIN
GOLDWAAGE	MUND	TON
HAARE	NAGEL	ZAUN
LINKS	OHREN	

Across

8. **viel um die _____ haben** *exp.* to be very busy, to be up to one's ears in work.

16. **_____ vergreifen (sich im)** *exp.* to blow it.

Down

9. **Keine grauen _____wachsen lassen (sich)** *exp.* not to lose sleep over something.

19. **Streit vom _____ brechen (einen)** *exp.* to start an argument.

27. **Wort auf die _____ legen (nicht jedes)** *exp.* to hang on one's every word.

30. **Dorn im _____ sein (jemandem ein)** *exp.* to be a thorn in one's side.

37. **_____ im Brett haben (bei jemandem einen)** *exp.* to be in one's good graces.

15. **_____ gefallen sein (nicht auf den)** *exp.* not to be at a loss for words.

17. **_____ auf den Kopf treffen (den)** *exp.* to be absolutely correct.

23. **_____ blasen (jemandem den)** *exp.* to reprimand someone.

28. **_____ liegen lassen (etwas)** *exp.* to pass something up.

CROSSWORD PUZZLE

B. Choose the correct word that completes the idiom.

1. Jemandem gehörig den Marsch (**pfeifen**, **blasen**, **singen**).

2. Sie hat mich die ganze Woche lang ohne Grund (**vorne**, **links**, **rechts**) liegen lassen.

3. Ich hatte heute soviel um die (**Augen**, **Ohren**, **Lippen**) bei der Arbeit.

4. Ich glaube, da hast du den Nagel auf den (**Arm**, **Hals**, **Kopf**) getroffen.

5. Die scheint ja ständig einen Streit vom Zaun zu (**reißen**, **schlagen**, **brechen**).

6. Ich lasse mir darüber keine (**weißen**, **grauen**, **schwarzen**) Haare wachsen.

7. Ich muß ihr wirklich ein Dorn im (**Ohr**, **Bein**, **Auge**) sein.

8. Vielleicht ist sie eifersüchtig, weil du bei allen anderen einen (**Stein**, **Fels**, **Kieselstein**) im Brett hast, und sie nicht.

C. Match the columns.

☐ 1. I got so busy at work today.

A. **Ich glaube, da hast du den Nagel auf den Kopf getroffen.**

☐ 2. If she puts me down at all, I'll give it to her!

B. **Ich muß ihr wirklich ein Dorn im Auge sein.**

☐ 3. She always seems to pick fights with you.

C. **Die scheint ja ständig einen Streit vom Zaun zu brechen.**

☐ 4. I think you hit the nail on the head.

D. **Sie hat mich die ganze Woche lang ohne Grund links liegen lassen.**

☐ 5. She gave me the cold shoulder all week for no reason.

E. **Du mußt wirklich lernen, nicht jedes ihrer Worte auf die Goldwaage zu legen.**

☐ 6. I must be a real thorn in her side.

F. **Wenn sie sich dann im Ton vergreift, werde ich ihr gehörig den Marsch blasen!**

☐ 7. Maybe she's jealous because you're in good graces with everyone and she's not.

G. **Ich hatte heute soviel um die Ohren bei der Arbeit.**

☐ 8. You really need to learn to take what she says with a grain of salt.

H. **Vielleicht ist sie eifersüchtig, weil du bei allen anderen einen Stein im Brett hast, und sie nicht.**

D. DICTATION 📼
Test Your Oral Comprehension

(This dictation can be found in Appendix A on page 174).

If you are following along with your cassette, you will now hear a series of sentences from the opening dialogue. These sentences will be read by a native speaker at normal conversational speed (which may seem fast to you at first). In addition, the words will be pronounced *as you would actually hear them in a conversation,* including many common reductions.

The first time the sentences are presented, simply listen in order to get accustomed to the speed and heavy use of reductions. The sentences will then be read again with a pause after each to give you time to write down what you heard. The third time the sentences are read, follow along with what you have written.

"ins Fettnäpfchen treten"

(trans): to put one's foot in one's mouth
(lit): to step in the fat bowl

Lektion Fünf

Am Strand

Kerstin: Was hältst du von meinem Badeanzug? Den habe ich schon seit meiner Schulzeit, und er **paßt mir immer noch wie angegossen.**

Birgit: Der sieht **klasse** aus. Es **würde mir nicht im Traum einfallen,** meinen zu tragen. Er würde mir niemals mehr passen. Ich würde nur in aller Öffentlichkeit **einen Narren aus mir machen.**

Kerstin: Nun sieh dir doch den Bikini da drüben an! Wie kann sie sowas nur tragen?! Ist sie **von allen guten Geistern verlassen**?

Birgit: Das ist Gretchen Berman. **Bei ihr ist eine Schraube locker.** Ich hoffe nur, sie sieht mich nicht. Wenn sie erst einmal **in Fahrt kommt,** hört sie so schnell nicht wieder auf zu erzählen. Und was sie sich immer so **aus den Fingern saugt, geht auf keine Kuhhaut.** Mir hat sie einmal **weismachen wollen,** daß sie Medizin studiert. Die kann doch nicht einmal einen Splitter rausziehen!

Kerstin: Ich erinnere mich an sie. Du hättest sie zwingen sollen, **Farbe zu bekennen.** Deine Mutter ist doch Ärztin. Sie hätte ihr ein paar ein paar medizinische Fragen stellen sollen. Ich kann gar nicht glauben, daß du dir so eine Gelegenheit **durch die Lappen gehen** lassen hast. Das wäre doch was gewesen, sie so **ins Fettnäpfchen treten** zu sehen.

Lesson Five

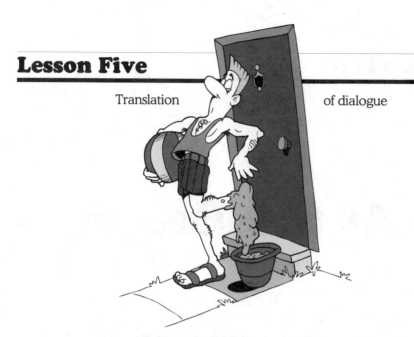

Translation of dialogue

Kerstin: What do you think of my bathing suit? I've had it since high school, and it still **fits like a glove**!

Birgit: It looks **great**. I wouldn't **dream of** wearing mine. It would never fit me anymore. I'd **make a fool of myself** in public.

Kerstin: Look at that bikini over there! How can she wear that? Has **she taken leave of her senses**?

Birgit: That's Gretchen Berman. She's **crazy**. I hope she doesn't see me. She'll **start talking** and never stop. She always **makes up unbelievable stories**, too. Once she tried **to pull the wool over my eyes by telling me** that she was studying to be a surgeon. She can't even take out a splinter!

Kerstin: I remember her. You should have **called her bluff**. Your mother is a doctor. You should have had your mother ask her some medical questions. I can't believe you let the chance **slip through your fingers**! It would have been great to watch her **put her foot in her mouth**.

Lesson Five

At the Beach

Kerstin: What do you think of my bathing suit? I've had it since high school, and it still **fits like cast on**.

Birgit: It looks **(first) class**. I **wouldn't think in a dream** of wearing mine. It would never fit me anymore. I'd **make a fool of myself** in public.

Kerstin: Well, look at that bikini over there! How can she wear that? Is she **being left by all good spirits**?

Birgit: That's Gretchen Berman. She's **got a screw loose**. I hope she doesn't see me. Once she **gets into full drive**, she won't stop talking. And whatever she **sucks out of her fingers won't fit on a cowhide**. She once tried to **do the wiser** telling me that she was studying to be a surgeon. She can't even take out a splinter!

Kerstin: I remember her. You should have made her **confess color**. Your mother is a doctor. You should have had your mother ask her some medical questions. I can't believe you let that chance **go through the rags**! It would have been great to watch her **step into the fat bowl**.

Vocabulary

angegossen passen (wie) *exp.* to fit like a glove • (lit); to fit as if something were cast on.

> usage example: Das Kleid ist genau die richtige Größe, es **paßt wie angegossen**!
>
> translation: This dress is the perfect size. It fits like a glove!
>
> literal translation: That dress is the perfect size. It fits as if it were cast on!

das geht auf keine Kuhhaut *exp.* to be beyond belief • (lit); it doesn't go on a cow hide.

> usage example: Wie der mit seinem neuen Auto angibt, **geht auf keine Kuhhaut mehr**.
>
> translation: The way he's bragging about his new car is really beyond belief.
>
> literal translation: The way he's bragging about his new car won't fit on a cow hide.

Fahrt kommen (in) *exp.* to get into full swing • (lit); come into full drive.

> usage example: Frag Opa bloß nicht nach Angelerlebnissen. Wenn er erst einmal **in Fahrt kommt**, hört er nicht wieder auf zu erzählen.
>
> translation: Don't ask grandpa to tell you his fishing stories. Once he starts, he won't stop for a long time.
>
> literal translation: Don't ask grandpa to tell you his fishing stories. Once he gets into full drive, he won't stop for a long time.

> OTHER IDIOMS USING "FAHRT":
> _____
>
> > **Fahrt bringen (jemanden in)** *exp.* to get someone all worked up • (lit); to bring someone in drive.
> >
> > **Fahrt ins Blaue machen (eine)** *exp.* to go for a drive • (lit); to make a drive into the blue.

freie Fahrt haben *exp.* to have been given the green light (to do something) • (lit); to have a free way.

voller Fahrt (in) *exp.* at full speed • (lit); in full drive.

Farbe bekennen müssen *exp.* to tell the truth, to "fess up", to lay one's cards on the table • (lit); to confess color.

usage example: Gerd mußte **Farbe bekennen**, daß er nicht über Computer bescheid weiß. Er hat gelogen, um den Job zu kriegen.

translation: Gerd had to lay his cards on the table that he really doesn't know anything about computers. He lied about it to get this job.

literal translation: Gerd had to confess color that he really doesn't know anything about computers. He lied about it to get this job.

Fettnäpfchen treten (ins) *exp.* to put one's foot in one's mouth • (lit); to step in the fat bowl.

usage example: Mit dieser Bemerkung bin ich ganz schön **ins Fettnäpfchen getreten**.

translation: I really put my foot in my mouth with that remark.

literal translation: I really stepped in the fat bowl with that remark.

Fingern saugen (sich etwas aus den) *exp.* to make something up • (lit); to suck something out of one's fingers.

usage example: Ela sagt, sie hätte Michael Jackson im Supermarket gesehen. Das hat sie sich sicher **aus den Fingern gesogen**.

translation: Ela said that she saw Michael Jackson at the supermarket. I'm sure she made that up.

literal translation: Ela said that she saw Michael Jackson at the supermarket. I'm sure she sucked that out of her fingers.

Finger geschnitten haben (sich in den) *exp.* to have another think coming • (lit); to have cut oneself in the finger.

Finger sehen/gucken (jemandem auf die) *exp.* to keep a sharp eye on someone • (lit); to see/look onto someone's fingers.

keinen Finger rühren *exp.* not to lift a finger • (lit); not to stir a finger.

kleinen Finger machen (etwas mit dem) *exp.* to do something with one's eyes shut • (lit); to do something with the little finger.

kleinen Finger wickeln (jemanden um den) *exp.* to wrap someone around one's little finger • (lit); to wrap someone around the little finger.

wenn man ihm den kleinen Finger reicht, nimmt er gleich die ganze Hand *exp.* give him an inch, he'll take a mile • (lit); if one extends the little finger to him, he'll take the whole hand.

Geistern verlassen sein (von allen guten) *exp.* to be out
of one's mind • (lit); to be left by all good spirits.

> usage example: Bist du **von allen guten Geistern verlassen**? Wenn der Chef dich beim Trinken bei der Arbeit erwischt, schmeißt er dich raus!
>
> translation: Are you out of your mind? If the boss sees you drinking on the job, he'll fire you!
>
> literal translation: Have you been left by all good spirits? If the boss sees you drinking on the job, he'll fire you!

klasse sein *exp.* to be first rate, great • (lit); to be (first) class.

> usage example: Wir hatten so viel Spaß bei der Wanderung. Es war einfach **klasse**!
>
> translation: We had so much fun hiking. It was just great!
>
> literal translation: We had so much fun hiking. It was just (first) class!

Lappen gehen (durch die) *exp.* to slip through someone's fingers, to give someone the slip • (lit); to get through the rags of someone.

> usage example: Die Schmugglerbande ist der Grenzpolizei **durch die Lappen gegangen**.
>
> translation: The gang of smugglers managed to slip through the fingers of the border police.
>
> literal translation: The gang of smugglers got through the rags of the border police.

Narren aus jemandem machen (einen) *exp.* to make a fool out of someone • (lit); [same].

> usage example: Warum bestehst du darauf, daß ich diese gräßliche Schlaghose anziehe? Willst du **einen Narren aus mir machen**?!
>
> translation: Why do you insist on me wearing those ugly bell bottom pants? Do you want me to look ridiculous?!
>
> literal translation: Why do you insist on me wearing those ugly bell bottom pants? Do you want to make a fool out of me?!

> OTHER IDIOMS USING "NARR":
> _____
>
> > **Narren gefressen haben an (etwas/ jemandem) (einen)** *exp.* to be infatuated with something/someone • (lit); to have eaten a fool on something/someone.
> >
> > **Narren halten (jemanden zum)** *exp.* to pull the wool over someone's eyes • (lit); to have/keep someone for a fool.

Schraube locker haben (eine) *exp.* to be crazy • (lit); to have a screw loose.

> usage example: Bei Petra ist doch **eine Schraube locker**. Sie geht am liebsten an den Strand wenn es regnet.
>
> translation: Petra's weird. She prefers going to the beach when it's raining.
>
> literal translation: Petra's got a screw loose. She prefers going to the beach when it's raining.

OTHER IDIOMS USING "SCHRAUBE":

Preise in die Höhe schrauben (die) *exp.* to push prices up • (lit); to screw or spiral prices in to heigher elevations.

Traum einfallen lassen (sich etwas nicht im) *exp.* to be inconceivable • (lit); not to think of doing something in one's dreams.

    usage example: Es würde mir **im Traum nicht einfallen**, mit Dieter auszugehen. Er ist so komisch!

    translation: I'd never consider of going out with Dieter. He's so weird!

    literal translation: I'd never dream of going out with Dieter. He's so weird!

weismachen wollen (jemandem/etwas) *exp.* to pull the wool over someone's eyes • (lit); to want to make someone/something wise.

    usage example: Marie **wollte mir weismachen**, daß ihre Familie königlicher Abstammung ist.

    translation: Marie tried to pull the wool over my eyes by telling me that her family is actually royalty.

    literal translation: Marie wanted to make me wise that her family is actually of royal descent.

Practice The Vocabulary

(Answers to Lesson 5, p. 165)

A. Choose the correct definition of the idiom.

1. **Fingern saugen (sich etwas aus den):**
   - ☐ a. to be out of one's mind
   - ☐ b. to make something up

2. **angegossen passen (wie):**
   - ☐ a. to fit like a glove
   - ☐ b. to tell the truth

3. **Geistern verlassen sein (von allen guten):**
   - ☐ a. to put one's foot in it
   - ☐ b. to be out of one's mind

4. **Fahrt kommen (in):**
   - ☐ a. to get into full swing
   - ☐ b. to be beyond belief

5. **Narren aus jemandem machen (einen):**
   - ☐ a. to make a fool out of someone
   - ☐ b. to be first rate

6. **Fettnäpfchen treten (ins):**
   - ☐ a. to slip through someone's fingers
   - ☐ b. to put one's foot in one's mouth

7. **das geht auf keine Kuhhaut:**
   - ☐ a. to be beyond belief
   - ☐ b. to make a fool out of someone

8. **klasse sein:**
   - ☐ a. to be first rate
   - ☐ b. to tell the truth

9. **Farbe bekennen müssen:**
   - ☐ a. to tell the truth
   - ☐ b. to put one's foot in it

10. **Lappen gehen (durch die):**
    - ☐ a. to make something up
    - ☐ b. to slip through someone's fingers

B. STEP 1: Circle the corresponding letter of the word that best completes the idiom.

STEP 2: Find your answer in the FIND-A-WORD cube on the opposite page.

1. Mit dieser Bemerkung bin ich ganz schön ins _____ getreten.
   a. **Fettnäpfchen**   b. **Mund**   c. **Schlamm**

2. Die Schmugglerbande ist der Grenzpolizei durch die _____ gegangen.
   a. **Hosen**   b. **Lumpen**   c. **Lappen**

3. Warum bestehst du darauf, daß ich diese gräßliche Schlaghose anziehe? Willst du einen _____ aus mir machen?
   a. **Schneider**   b. **Bäcker**   c. **Narren**

4. Wie er mit seinem neuen Auto angibt, geht auf keine _____ mehr.
   a. **Kuhhaut**   b. **Ziege**   c. **Schafshaut**

5. Wir hatten so viel Spaß bei der Wanderung. Es war einfach _____!
   a. **doof**   b. **egal**   c. **klasse**

6. Bei Petra ist doch eine _____ locker!
   a. **Mutter**   b. **Schraube**   c. **Heftzwecke**

7. Mir hat sie einmal weismachen _____, daß sie Chirurgie studiert.
   a. **wollen**   b. **dürfen**   c. **müssen**

8. Ela sagt, sie hätte Michael Jackson im Supermarkt gesehen. Das hat sie sich sicher aus den _____ gesaugt.
   a. **Zehen**   b. **Fingern**   c. **Augen**

FIND-A-WORD PUZZLE

```
A F N K U H H A U T W E T
F E F S M B R Ä O A A W A
Ü T F I N G E R N D S O N
N T O I S E M N A O S L S
F N B E C K T C N T O L C
T Ä I S H B I L D E R E H
E P R L A P P E N S C N R
X F E A U L C N A C H E A
B C L O B K E D R A E J U
A H A A E A A R R R N E B
L E L H Ü H N C E E N T E
I N Y O T E O Ö N E U A W
S O K L A S S E R S T I Ü
```

C. Match the columns.

☐ 1. You should have called her bluff.

☐ 2. It still fits like a glove.

☐ 3. It looks great.

☐ 4. Once she tried to trick me into believing that she was studying to be a surgeon.

☐ 5. I can't believe you let the chance slip through your fingers.

☐ 6. She's crazy.

☐ 7. Once she starts, she won't stop for a long time.

☐ 8. It would have been great to watch her put her foot in her mouth.

A. **Bei ihr ist doch eine Schraube locker.**

B. **Wenn sie erstmal in Fahrt kommt, hört sie so schnell nicht wieder auf zu erzählen.**

C. **Mir hat sie einmal weismachen wollen, daß sie Medizin studiert.**

D. **Du hättest sie zwingen sollen, Farbe zu bekennen.**

E. **Ich kann gar nicht glauben, daß du dir so eine Gelegenheit durch die Lappen gehen lassen hast.**

F. **Er paßt mir immer noch wie angegossen.**

G. **Der sieht klasse aus.**

H. **Das wäre doch toll gewesen, sie so ins Fettnäpfchen treten zu sehen.**

D. DICTATION 🔲
Test Your Oral Comprehension

(This dictation can be found in Appendix A on page 174).

If you are following along with your cassette, you will now hear a series of sentences from the opening dialogue. These sentences will be read by a native speaker at normal conversational speed (which may seem fast to you at first). In addition, the words will be pronounced *as you would actually hear them in a conversation*, including many common reductions.

The first time the sentences are presented, simply listen in order to get accustomed to the speed and heavy use of reductions. The sentences will then be read again with a pause after each to give you time to write down what you heard. The third time the sentences are read, follow along with what you have written.

REVIEW EXAM FOR LESSONS 1-5

(Answers to Review, p. 167)

A. Underline the appropriate word that best completes the phrase.

1. Es wundert mich nicht, daß Kurt und Hanna heiraten. Sie waren schon in der Schule immer (**eine Lunge**, **eine Niere**, **ein Herz**) und eine Seele.

2. Du nimmst immer Schmalz statt Butter?! Na, da liegt doch (**das Eichhörnchen**, **die Ente**, **der Hund**) begraben. Deshalb werden deine Kuchen nichts.

3. Ich muß dir ein Geheimnis anvertrauen. Können wir irgendwo unter vier (**Augen**, **Ohren**, **Narren**) sprechen?

4. Du solltest doch nicht an die große (**Klingel**, **Glocke**, **Sirene**) hängen, daß ich schwanger bin. Ich habe es meinen Eltern doch noch nicht erzählt!

5. Andrea geht das Wochenende zum Zelten? Du willst mich wohl auf den (**Arm**, **Bein**, **Nase**) nehmen. Sie hat doch Platzangst. Sie schläft doch niemals in einem Zelt!

6. Ich ärgere mich grün und (**rot**, **orange**, **blau**), daß ich diese Woche kein Lotto gespielt habe. All meine Zahlen wurden gezogen!

7. Ich glaube, du hast den Nagel auf den (**Ohr**, **Arm**, **Kopf**) getroffen als du sagtest, der Film sei völlig idiotisch.

8. Hubert hat sich wirklich im (**Lied**, **Melodie**, **Ton**) vergriffen, als er seinen Chef einen Idioten nannte.

B. CROSSWORD

Step 1: Fill in the blanks with the appropriate word(s) from the list below.

Step 2: Using your answers, fill in the crossword puzzle on page 83.

AUGE	FARBE	KUHHAUT
AUGEN	FASSUNG	LAPPEN
BILD	GEISTERN	LAUS
BREI	GLOCKE	SCHNALLEN
BRETT	HAARE	SCHNITZER
BUCHE	HALS	SCHRAUBE
DENKZETTEL	HAUT	SPIEß
DORN	HÜHNCHEN	WORT

Across

11. Mein kleiner Bruder hat schon wieder mein Auto geliehen ohne zu fragen. Diesmal werde ich ihm aber einen _____ verpassen!

17. Du hast mich völlig aus der _____ gebracht mit deinen Bemerkungen über meine Figur!

22. Helmut hat mich beschuldigt, unnötig viel Wasser beim Duschen zu verbrauchen. Da habe ich den _____ einfach umgedreht, und ihn an sein stundenlanges Autowaschen erinnert.

24. Ich möchte wirklich nicht in deiner _____ stecken, wenn Mutti rausfindet, daß du ihr Auto geschrottet hast.

28. Unsere Lehrerin hat uns die Matheaufgabe nochmal erklärt, aber Eva und Anette _____ sie immer noch nicht.

40. Mein Vater hat bei meiner Oma einen Stein im _____ , weil er ihr immer im Garten hilft.

43. Jochen hat den ganzen Nachmittag in der Schlammpfütze gespielt — ein _____ für die Götter!

50. Bei Petra ist doch eine _____ locker. Sie geht am liebsten an den Strand, wenn es regnet.

62. Die Schmugglerbande ist der Grenzpolizei durch die _____ gegangen.

Down

7. Bist du von allen guten _____ verlassen? Wenn der Chef dich beim trinken bei der Arbeit erwischt, schmeißt er dich raus!

11. Ich bin froh, daß wir endlich unser Haus streichen. Die alte Farbe war mir schon immer ein _____ im Auge.

12. Wie er mit seinem neuen Auto angibt, geht auf keine _____ mehr.

13. Der Verkehrspolizist hat nochmal ein _____ zugedrückt und mir keinen Strafzettel gegeben.

20. Mit dir habe ich noch ein _____ zu rupfen, Lise. Wie kommt der Brandfleck in das neue Kleid, das ich dir geborgt hatte?!

24. Was ich über seine Frau gesagt habe, hat er völlig in den falschen _____ gekriegt.

26. Du solltest doch nicht an die große _____ hängen, daß ich schwanger bin. Ich habe es meinen Eltern noch nicht erzählt!

28. Da habe ich mir einen groben _____ erlaubt, als
    ich versuchte, diese junge Frau auf der Party zu küssen. Es stellte
    sich heraus, daß es die Frau vom Chef war!

29. Man sagt, daß wir eines Tages ein grosses Erdbeben haben
    werden, aber darüber lasse ich mir keine grauen _____
    wachsen. Wenn es passiert, passiert es eben.

30. Ich muß dir eine geheime Sache anvertrauen. Können wir
    irgendwo unter vier _____ sprechen?

38. In einem Scheidungsfall wird jedes _____ auf die
    Goldwaage gelegt.

43. Sag mir einfach was du willst! Hör auf um den heißen _____
    zu reden!

44. Lena hat den ganzen Tag noch nicht ein einziges Mal gelächelt.
    Was ihr wohl für eine _____ über die Leber gelaufen ist?

47. Marion ist eine Verkäuferin wie sie im _____ steht. Sie
    hat diese Woche dreimal mehr verkauft, als ihre Mitarbeiterinnen.

58. Gerd mußte _____ bekennen, daß er nicht über
    Computer bescheid weiss. Er hat gelogen, um den Job zu kriegen.

CROSSWORD PUZZLE

C. Choose the correct translation of the German sentence.

1. **Was ist dir nur für eine Laus über die Leber gelaufen?**
   - ☐ a. What's eating you?
   - ☐ b. Why are you so bored?

2. **Angela geht mir so auf die Nerven!**
   - ☐ a. Angela always yells at me!
   - ☐ b. Angela really gets on my nerves!

3. **Ins Museum zu gehen, langweilt mich zu Tode.**
   - ☐ a. I love going to museums.
   - ☐ b. Going to museums bores me to death.

4. **Ich fühl mich wie das fünfte Rad am Wagen.**
   - ☐ a. I feel like I belong here.
   - ☐ b. I feel out of place here.

5. **Ihr werde ich die Leviten lesen!**
   - ☐ a. I'm going to give her a big hug!
   - ☐ b. I'm going to read her the riot act!

6. **Dein Schweigen kann ich nicht länger ertragen. Laß uns das Geschehene besprechen und reinen Tisch machen.**
   - ☐ a. I can't stand your silence any longer. Let's talk about what happened and clear the air.
   - ☐ b. I can't stand your silence any longer. I don't want to be friends any more.

7. **Ich habe so die Nase von ihm voll.**
   - ☐ a. I really like him.
   - ☐ b. I'm fed up with him.

8. **Du nimmst mich doch auf den Arm!**
   - ☐ a. You're pulling my leg!
   - ☐ b. You look so ticked off!

9. **Stephan kann einfach nichts Süßes links liegen lassen.**
   - ☐ a. Stephan can't stand sweets.
   - ☐ b. Stephan can't pass up sweets.

10. **Hubert hat sich wirklich im Ton vergriffen, als er seinen Chef einen Idioten nannte.**
    - ☐ a. Hubert really blew it when he called his boss an idiot.
    - ☐ b. Hurbert was just kidding when he called his boss an idiot.

11. **Wie er mit seinem neuen Auto angibt geht auf keine Kuhhaut mehr.**
    - ☐ a. The way he's bragging about his new car is really cute.
    - ☐ b. The way he's bragging about his new car is really beyond belief.

12. **Frag Opa bloß nicht nach Angelerlebnissen. Wenn er erstmal in Fahrt kommt, hört er nicht wieder auf zu erzählen.**
    - ☐ a. Don't ask grandpa to tell you his fishing stories. Once he starts, he won't stop for a long time.
    - ☐ b. Don't ask grandpa to tell you his fishing stories. Once he starts, he tends to lose his train of thought.

13. **Wir hatten so viel Spaß bei der Wanderung. Es war einfach klasse!**
    - ☐ a. We had so much fun hiking. It was just great!
    - ☐ b. We had so much fun hiking. It was exhausting, though!

14. **Die Schmugglerbande ist der Grenzpolizei durch die Lappen gegangen.**
    - ☐ a. The gang of smugglers managed to slip through the fingers of the border police.
    - ☐ b. The gang of smugglers got caught by the border police.

"Da bleibt mir ja die Spucke weg"

(trans): to be speechless
(lit): my saliva stays away

Dialogue in slang

Im Supermarkt

Matthias: Guck mal! Ist das nicht Klaus an der Kasse? Er war doch mal Direktor der größten Sparkasse in der Stadt. **Da bleibt mir ja die Spucke weg**!

Michel: Ich weiß. Er hat all sein Geld an der Börse verloren. Den einen Tag hat er **Geld wie Heu**, den anderen Tag ist er **arm wie eine Kirchenmaus**. Warum mußte er auch **alles auf eine Karte setzen**? Ich **gehe immer auf Nummer sicher**, wenn ich Geld in irgend etwas investiere.

Matthias: Das ist ja wirklich **in die Hose gegangen**. Na, nach sowas kann man nur **die Ohren steif halten** und **darf die Flinte nicht ins Korn werfen**.

Michel: Er sieht auch ganz zufrieden aus. Ich schätze, er **schiebt hier eine etwas ruhigere Kugel** als bei einer großen Bank.

Matthias: Kassierer zu sein ist nicht so einfach wie es aussieht. Dafür muß man ganz schön **auf Draht sein**.

Michel: (Witzelnd) Deshalb warst du nie Kassierer!

Lesson Six

Matthias: Look! Isn't that Klaus working at the cash register? He used to be the president of the biggest bank in the city. I'm **flabbergasted**!

Michel: I know. He lost all of his money in the stock market. One day he was **rich** and the next day he was **broke**. Why would he **put all his eggs in one basket** like that? I always **play it safe** when I invest my money in anything.

Matthias: His whole life just **went up in smoke**. Well, after something like that, all you can do is to keep a **stiff upper lip** and not **throw in the towel**.

Michel: He sure does look happy. I guess he has **it easy** working here compared to a big bank.

Matthias: Being a cashier isn't as easy as it looks. You really have to **be on the ball**.

Michel: (Jokingly) So that's why you've never been a cashier!

Lesson Six

At the Market

Matthias: Look! Isn't that Klaus working at the cash register? He used to be the president of the biggest bank in the city. That **leaves me without spit**!

Michel: I know. He lost all of his money in the stock market. One day he's got **money like hay** and the next day he's **poor as a churchmouse**. Why would he **bet all on one card**? I always go **on number safe** when I invest my money in anything.

Matthias: That really **went into the pants**. Well, after something like that, all you can do is **to keep the ears stiff** and **not to throw the rifle in the corn**.

Michel: He sure does look happy. I guess, he's **pushing a calmer sphere** here, compared to a big bank.

Matthias: Being a cashier isn't as easy as it looks. You really have to be **on wire**.

Michel: (Jokingly) So that's why you've never been a cashier!

Vocabulary

arm wie eine Kirchenmaus sein *exp.* to be dirt poor • (lit); to be as poor as a church mouse.

    usage example: Es ist schwer zu glauben, daß Lydia mal **arm wie eine Kirchenmaus** war. Heute hat sie mehrere Geschäfte.

    translation: It's hard to believe that Lydia used to be dirt poor. Today she owns several businesses.

    literal translation: It's hard to believe that Lydia used to be as poor as a church mouse. Today she owns several businesses.

Da bleibt mir ja die Spucke weg *exp.* to be speechless • (lit); to be spitless.

    usage example: Seeligman ist befördert worden?! **Da bleibt mir ja die Spucke weg**!

    translation: Seeligman got a promotion?! I'm speechless!

    literal translation: Seeligman got a promotion?! That leaves me spitless!

Draht sein (auf) *exp.* to be on one's toes • (lit); to be on wire.

    usage example: Als Feuerwehrmann muß man immer **auf Draht sein**.

    translation: As a firefighter, you always have to be on your toes.

    literal translation: As a firefighter, you always have to be on wire.

OTHER IDIOMS USING "DRAHT":

    heißer Draht *exp.* hot line • (lit); hot wire.

Flinte nicht ins Korn werfen (die) *exp.* not to throw in the towel • (lit); not to throw the rifle into the corn (field).

    usage example: Du darfst einfach **nicht die Flinte ins Korn werfen**. Irgendwann wirst du die Führerscheinprüfung schon bestehen.

    translation: You can't just throw in the towel. You'll pass the driver's test eventually.

    literal translation: You can't just throw the rifle into the corn (field). You'll pass the driver's test eventually.

Geld wie Heu haben *exp.* to be filthy rich • (lit); to have money like hay.

    usage example: Lothar **hat Geld wie Heu**. Er kauft sich jedes Jahr ein neues Auto!

    translation: Lothar is filthy rich. He buys a new car every year!

    literal translation: Lothar's got money like hay. He buys a new car every year!

OTHER IDIOMS USING "GELD":

    das ist hinausgeworfenes Geld *exp.* that's money down the drain • (lit); that's thrown out money.

    Geld machen (etwas zu) *exp.* to turn something into cash • (lit); to make something into money.

    Geld scheffeln *exp.* to rake in the money • (lit); to shovel money.

    Gelde schwimmen (im) *exp.* to be rolling in money • (lit); to be swimming in money.

    große Geld machen (das) *exp.* to make a lot of money • (lit); to make the big money.

Hose gehen (in die) *exp.* not to turn out well • (lit); to go into the pants.

    usage example: Meine Zeichnung für den Kunstunterricht ist völlig **in die Hose gegangen**. Es sollte ein Mädchen sein, aber es sieht aus wie eine Birne.

translation: My drawing for art class didn't turn out well. It was supposed to be a girl but it looks like a pear!

literal translation: My drawing for art class went into the pants. It was supposed to be a girl but it looks like a pear!

OTHER IDIOMS USING "HOSE":

Hosen anhaben (die) *exp.* to have the upper hand • (lit); to have the pants on.

Hosenboden setzen (sich auf den) *exp.* to get down to work • (lit); to sit down on one's pants.

Hosen strammziehen (jemandem die) *exp.* to give someone a spanking • (lit); to straighten someone's pants.

Hosen voll haben (die) *exp.* to be scared • (lit); to have the pants full.

Karte setzen (alles auf eine) *exp.* to put all one's eggs into one basket • (lit); to bet it all on one card.

usage example: Setze nicht **alles auf eine Karte**! Du solltest dich noch um andere Jobs bemühen, für den Fall, daß du diesen nicht kriegen solltest.

translation: Don't put all your eggs into one basket! You really should apply for some other jobs in case you don't get this one.

literal translation: Don't bet it all on one card! You really should apply for some other jobs in case you don't get this one.

OTHER IDIOMS USING "KARTE":

Karten aufdecken (seine) *exp.* to show one's hand • (lit); to expose one's cards.

gute Karten haben *exp.* to have a good chance • (lit); to have good cards.

Karten sehen (jemandem) (in die) *exp.* to see through someone's game • (lit); to look in someone's cards.

offenen Karten spielen (mit) *exp.* to put one's cards on the table • (lit); to play with open cards.

Nummer sicher gehen (auf) *exp.* to be on the safe side • (lit); to get to number safe.

usage example: Bevor du deinen Aufsatz abgibst, lies ihn dir lieber nochmal durch, um **auf Nummer sicher zu gehen**.

translation: Before you hand in your essay to the teacher, you'd better proofread it again just to be on the safe side.

literal translation: Before you hand in your essay to the teacher, you'd better proofread it again just to get to number safe.

OTHER IDIOMS USING "NUMMER":

etwas/jemand is eine Nummer zu groß für dich *exp.* said of someone who bites off more than he can chew • (lit); something/someone is one number too big for you.

Nummer sein (eine) *exp.* to be quite a number, to be a real character • (lit); to be a number.

Ohren steif halten (die) *exp.* to keep a stiff upper lip • (lit); to keep the ears stiff.

usage example: Ich bin sicher, daß die Polizei deinen Bruder finden wird. **Halt die Ohren steif** und hoffe auf das Beste.

translation: I'm sure the police will find your brother. Keep a stiff upper lip and hope for the best.

literal translation: I'm sure the police will find your brother. Keep the ears stiff and hope for the best.

OTHER IDIOMS USING "OHR":

"Es ist mir zu Ohren gekommen" *exp.* "It has come to my attention" • (lit); It has come to my ears

"Mir klingen die Ohren." *exp.* "My ears are ringing." • (lit); My ears are sounding.

bis über beide Ohren verliebt sein in jemanden *exp.* to be head over heels in love with someone • (lit); to be in love with someone over both ears.

bis über die Ohren *exp.* to be up to one's ears (in something) • (lit); up over the ears.

Bohnen/Petersilie in den Ohren haben *exp.* to turn a deaf ear to something • (lit); to have beans/parsley in the ears.

ganz Ohr sein *exp.* to be all ears • (lit); to be all ear.

grün hinter den Ohren sein *exp.* to be wet behind the ears • (lit); to be green behind the ears.

offenes Ohr finden (ein) *exp.* to find a sympathetic ear • (lit); to find an open ear.

Ohr haben für etwas (ein) *exp.* to have an ear for something • (lit); [same].

Ohr hinein, zum andern hinaus (zum einen) *exp.* in one ear and out the other • (lit); [same].

Ohr legen (sich aufs) *exp.* to take a nap • (lit); to lie on one's ear.

Ohr zum andern grinsen (von einem) *exp.* to smile from ear to ear • (lit); to grin from one ear to the other.

Ohren hängen lassen (die) *exp.* to lose heart • (lit); to leave the ears hanging.

Ohren liegen (jemandem in den) *exp.* to bug someone relentlessly about something • (lit); to lie in someone's ears.

Ohren spitzen (die) *exp.* to prick up one's ears • (lit); to sharpen one's ears.

tauben Ohren predigen (vor) *exp.* to preach to deaf ears • (lit); [same].

übers Ohr hauen (jemanden) *exp.* to put one over on someone • (lit); to hit someone over the ear.

Wände haben Ohren (die) *exp.* the walls have ears • (lit); [same].

ruhige Kugel schieben (eine) *exp.* to kick back and relax • (lit); to push a calm ball.

> usage example: Am Sonntag habe ich nichts zu tun. Ich glaube, da werde **ich eine ruhige Kugel schieben**.
>
> translation: I've got nothing to do on Sunday. I think I'll just kick back and relax.
>
> literal translation: I've got nothing to do on Sunday. I think I'll just push a calm ball.

Practice The Vocabulary

(Answers to Lesson 6, p. 168)

A. Choose the correct word that completes the idiom.

1. Das ist ja wirklich in die (**Jacke, Hose, Hemd**) gegangen.

2. Da bleibt mir ja die (**Rotze, Stimme, Spucke**) weg!

3. Kassierer zu sein ist nicht so einfach, wie es aussieht. Dafür muß man ganz schön auf (**Draht, Kabel, Schnur**) sein.

4. Ich habe Geld wie (**Heu, Stroh, Weizen**).

5. Nach so etwas kann man nur die (**Beine, Haare, Ohren**) steif halten.

6. Warum mußte er auch alles auf eine (**Nummer, Karte, Farbe**) setzen?

7. Er sieht auch ganz zufrieden aus. Ich schätze, er schiebt hier eine etwas ruhigere (**Kreis, Ball, Kugel**).

8. Ich gehe immer auf (**Nummer, Zahl, Farbe**) sicher, wenn ich Geld in irgend etwas investiere.

B. FIND-A-WORD CUBE
Find the answers from Exercise B in the cube below.

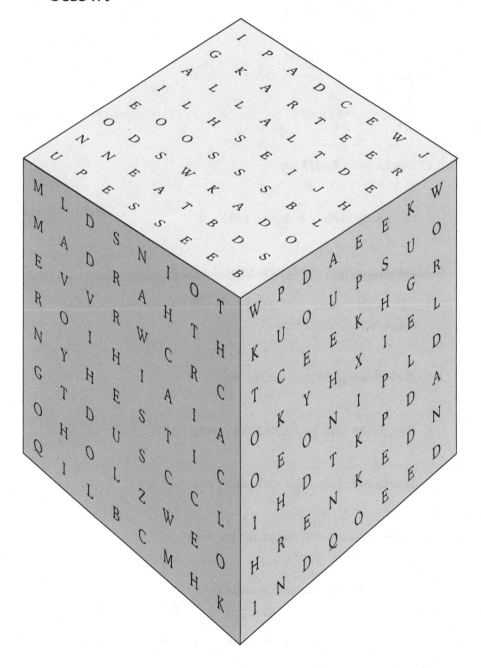

C. Choose the definition that goes with the idiom.

A. to be rich
B. to be speechless
C. to kick back and relax
D. to put all one's eggs into one basket
E. to be on one's toes

F. to be dirt poor
G. to keep a stiff upper lip
H. to be on the safe side
I. to throw in the towel
J. to turn out badly

☐ 1. **Draht sein (auf)** *exp.*

☐ 2. **Nummer sicher gehen (auf)** *exp.*

☐ 3. **ruhige Kugel schieben (eine)** *exp.*

☐ 4. **Geld wie Heu haben** *exp.*

☐ 5. **Ohren steif halten (die)** *exp.*

☐ 6. **Da bleibt mir ja die Spucke weg** *exp.*

☐ 7. **Karte setzen (alles auf eine)** *exp.*

☐ 8. **Hose gegangen (etwas ist in die)** *exp.*

☐ 9. **arm wie eine Kirchenmaus sein** *exp.*

☐ 10. **Flinte ins Korn werfen (die)** *exp.*

D. DICTATION 📼
Test Your Oral Comprehension

(This dictation can be found in Appendix A on page 174).

If you are following along with your cassette, you will now hear a series of sentences from the opening dialogue. These sentences will be read by a native speaker at normal conversational speed (which may seem fast to you at first). In addition, the words will be pronounced *as you would actually hear them in a conversation*, including many common reductions.

The first time the sentences are presented, simply listen in order to get accustomed to the speed and heavy use of reductions. The sentences will then be read again with a pause after each to give you time to write down what you heard. The third time the sentences are read, follow along with what you have written.

"jemandem ist das Herz total in die Hose gerutscht"

(trans): *to have one's heart in one's throat*
(lit): *someone's heart has totally slid in his pants*

Lektion Sieben

Ein Ski Ausflug

Phillip: **Spitze**! Das Wetter heute ist einfach **zu schön um wahr zu sein**. Na, bist du fertig für deinen ersten Abfahrtslauf?!

Stefan: Machst du Witze? Ich will ja kein **Spielverderber** sein, aber mir ist **das Herz total in die Hose gerutscht**! Ich glaube nicht, daß ich schon soweit bin, **Kopf und Kragen zu riskieren**. Du magst diesen Sport sehr, nicht?

Phillip: Ja, **darauf kannst du Gift nehmen**! Es ist wirklich einfach. Du **hast den Bogen** in **Nullkommanix raus**. Die Sache **hat nur einen Haken** — wenn du über einen Stein fährst, kannst du plötzlich stolpern und fallen. Aber laß dich nicht entmutigen. Du mußt einfach **bei der Stange bleiben**, um besser zu werden. Oh, und wenn du mit jemandem zusammenstößt und dir einen Knochen brichst, gibt es eine Erstehilfehütte am Fuß des Berges. O.K., **jetzt geht's um die Wurst**! Einfach **Daumen drücken**, daß du nicht aus Versehen über die Klippe fährst, wie ich letzte Woche. **Hals und Beinbruch**!

Lesson Seven

Translation of dialogue

Phillip: **Wow**! The weather today is just **too good to be true**. Well, are you ready for your first day of downhill skiing?

Stefan: Are you kidding? I don't want **to be a kill-joy**, but I'm **scared to death**! I don't think I'm ready **to risk my neck**. You really like this sport, don't you?

Phillip: **You bet your life**! It's really easy. You'll get the **hang of it in no time**. There's just one **snag** — if you ski over a rock, you may stop suddenly and fall. But don't let it discourage you. You've got **to stick to it** in order to improve. Oh, and if someone crashes into you and you break a bone, there's a first aid station at the bottom of the mountain. Okay, it's **now or never**! Just **keep your fingers crossed** that you don't accidentally ski off the cliff like I did last week. **Break a leg**!

Literal translation of dialogue

A Skiing Trip

Phillip: **Peak**! The weather today is **too beautiful to be true**. Well, are you ready for your first day of downhill skiing?

Stefan: Are you kidding? I don't want **to be a kill-joy**, but **my heart totally slipped down my pants**! I don't think I'm ready to **risk my head and neck**. You really like this sport, don't you?

Phillip: **You can take poison on that**! You'll **get the curve** in **zero comma nothing**. The thing's **got only one hook** — if you ski over a rock, you may stop suddenly and fall. But don't let it discourage you. You've got **to stay at the pole** in order to improve. Oh, and if someone crashes into you and you break a bone, there's a first aid station at the bottom of the mountain. Okay, now **it's for the sausage**! Just **press your thumbs** that you don't accidentally ski off the cliff like I did last week. **Neck and leg fracture**!

Vocabulary

Bogen raushaben (den) *exp.* to get the hang of something • (lit); to get the arch on something.

> usage example: Ich habe jetzt endlich **den Bogen raus**, wie man einen Reifen wechselt.

> translation: I finally got the hang of changing a tire.

> literal translation: I finally got the curve on how to change a tire.

> OTHER IDIOMS USING "BOGEN":

>> **Bogen überspannen (den)** *exp.* to go too far • (lit); to overstretch the bow.

>> **großen Bogen um jemanden machen (einen)** *exp.* to stay clear of someone • (lit); to make a big arc around someone.

Daumen drücken (jemandem die) *exp.* to keep one's fingers crossed for someone • (lit); to keep one's thumbs pressed for someone.

> usage example: Morgen werde ich meinen Chef um eine Gehaltserhöhung bitten. **Drück mir ganz fest die Daumen**!

> translation: Tomorrow I'm going to ask my boss for a raise. Keep your fingers crossed for me!

> literal translation: Tomorrow I'm going to ask my boss for a raise. Please press your thumbs real hard for me!

> OTHER IDIOMS USING "DAUMEN":

>> **Daumen peilen (über den)** *exp.* roughly, approximately • (lit); over the thumb.

Daumen drehen (die) *exp.* to twiddle one's thumbs • (lit); to turn the thumbs.

Daumen halten (jemanden) (unter dem) *exp.* to keep someone under one's thumb • (lit); [same].

die Sache hat einen Haken *exp.* there's one hitch • (lit); the matter has one hook.

    usage example: Das Jobangebot ist wirklich gut. Es hat nur **einen Haken** — Ich müßte nach Grönland ziehen.

    translation: The job offer is really good. There's only one hitch. I'd have to move to Greenland.

    literal translation: The job offer is really good. It has only one hook. I'd have to move to Greenland.

es geht um die Wurst *exp.* to be do or die, now or never • (lit); it's about the sausage.

    usage example: Alle drei Tennisspieler halten den selben Punktestand. Das nächste Spiel bestimmt den Gewinner. Jetzt **geht's um die Wurst**!

    translation: Both tennis players are tied. The next game will determine the winner of the match. It's do or die!

    literal translation: Both tennis players are tied. The next game will determine the winner of the match. It's for the sausage!

OTHER IDIOMS USING "WURST":

Es ist mir (ganz) Wurst *exp.* I don't give a hoot. • (lit); It's a (total) sausage to me.

etwas ist zu schön, um wahr zu sein *exp.* to be too good to be true • (lit); [same].

usage example: Ich wünschte, wir könnten ein einziges Mad fliegen, ohne Ärger mit dem Gepäck zu haben. Das wäre doch **zu schön, um wahr zu sein**.

translation: Just once, I wish we could take a plane trip and not have any trouble with the luggage. That would be too good to be true.

literal translation: [same].

Gift nehmen können (auf etwas) *exp.* to bet one's bottom dollar on something • (lit); to take poison on something.

usage example: "Willst du wirlich deinen Job kündigen?"
"Darauf **kannst du Gift nehmen**! Ich kann meinen Chef nicht mehr ausstehen!"

translation: "Do you really want to quit your job?"
"You better believe it! I can't tolerate my boss any longer!"

literal translation: "Do you really want to quit your job?"
"You can take poison on that! I can't tolerate my boss any longer!"

Hals und Beinbruch wünschen (jemandem) *exp.* to wish someone good luck ("Break a leg!") • (lit); to wish someone a neck and leg fracture ("Neck and leg fracture!").

usage example: Ich höre du hast morgen ein Vorstellungsgespräch. Ich wünsche dir **Hals und Beinbruch**!

translation: I hear you have a job interview tomorrow. Break a leg!

literal translation: I hear you have a job interview tomorrow. Neck and leg fracture!

OTHER IDIOMS USING "HALS":

SEE: *page 5.*

Herz total in die Hose gerutscht (jemandem ist das)

exp. to have one's heart in one's throat • (lit); someone's heart has totally slid in his plants.

usage example: Als ich letzte Nacht Schritte im Haus gehört habe, ist mir **das Herz total in die Hose gerutscht**.

translation: When I heard footsteps in my house last night, my heart suddenly went into my throat.

literal translation: When I heard footsteps in my house last night, my heart suddenly slipped in my pants.

OTHER IDIOMS USING "HERZ":

SEE: *page 6.*

Kopf und Kragen riskieren *exp.* to risk life and limb • (lit); to risk head and neck.

usage example: Hans ist ein Polizist. Er **riskiert täglich Kopf und Kragen**.

translation: Hans is a police officer. He risks life and limb everyday.

literal translation: Hans is a police officer. He risks his head and neck everyday.

OTHER IDIOMS USING "KOPF":

SEE: *page 56.*

Spielverderber sein *exp.* to be a kill-joy • (lit); to be a game-spoiler.

usage example: Mußt du so ein **Spielverderber** sein? Warum hast du die Musik ausgemacht? Wir hatten soviel Spaß beim Tanzen.

translation: Do you have to be such a kill-joy? Why did you turn the music off? We were having so much fun dancing.

literal translation: Do you have to be such a game-spoiler? Why did you turn the music off? We were having so much fun dancing.

spitze *exp.* the best • (lit); the peak.

    usage example: Das Rolling Stones Konzert war einfach **spitze**!

    translation: The Rolling Stones concert was totally awsome!

    literal translation: The Rolling Stones concert was the absolute peak!

OTHER IDIOMS USING "SPITZE":

    Spitze liegen (an der) *exp.* to be in the lead, first place (sports) • (lit); to lie at the peak.

    Spitze treiben etwas (auf die) *exp.* to carry things too far • (lit); to drive to the peak of something.

Stange bleiben (bei der) *exp.* to stick to doing something • (lit); to stay at the pole.

    usage example: Du kannst schon einige Lieder auf der Gitarre spielen, und wenn du jetzt **bei der Stange** bleibst, spielst du bald wie ein Profi!

    translation: You're starting to play the guitar very well. If you stick to it, some day you'll be able to play like a pro!

    literal translation: You're starting to play the guitar very well. If you stay at the pole, some day you'll be able to play like a pro!

OTHER IDIOMS USING "STANGE":

    Bohnenstange *exp.* tall person • (lit); bean pole.

    schöne Stange Geld (eine) *exp.* a nice sum of money • (lit); a nice pole of money.

    Stange (von der) *exp.* off-the-rack • (lit); off the pole.

    Stange halten (jemandem) (die) *exp.* to stick up for someone • (lit); to hold someone's pole.

Practice The Vocabulary

(Answers to Lesson 7, p. 169)

A. Choose the correct word that completes the idiom.

1. (**Gipfel**, **Grund**, **Spitze**)! Das war wunderbar!

2. Ich höre, du hast morgen ein Vorstellungsgespräch. Ich wünsche dir (**Arm**, **Hals**, **Nase**) und Beinbruch!

3. Das Wetter heute ist einfach zu schön um (**wahr**, **wirklich**, **falsch**) zu sein.

4. Beide Tennisspieler halten denselben Punktestand. Das nächste Spiel bestimmt den Gewinner. Jetzt geht's um die (**Suppe**, **Schinken**, **Wurst**)!

5. "Du magst diesen Sport sehr, nicht?"
   "Ja, darauf kannst du (**Schnaps**, **Vitamine**, **Gift**) nehmen!"

6. Du mußt einfach bei der (**Stange**, **Balken**, **Stock**) bleiben, um besser zu werden.

7. Mir ist das Herz total in die (**Schuhe**, **Tasche**, **Hose**) gerutscht.

8. Einfach (**Daumen**, **Finger**, **Füße**) drücken, daß du nicht aus Versehen über die Klippe fährst.

B. CROSSWORD
Complete the dialogue below by choosing the missing word in the idiom. Then, fill in the crossword puzzle on the opposite page with the word you have chosen.

BOGEN	HERZ	STANGE
DAUMEN	KRAGEN	WAHR
GIFT	NULLKOMMANIX	WURST
HAKEN	SPIELVERDERBER	
HALS	SPITZE	

Phillip: **[17A]** _____ ! Das Wetter heute ist einfach zu schön um **[1A]** _____ zu sein. Na, bist du fertig für deinen ersten Abfahrtslauf?!

Stefan: Machst du Witze? Ich will ja kein **[12D]** _____ sein, aber mir ist das **[42D]** _____ total in die Hose gerutscht! Ich glaube nicht, daß ich schon soweit bin, Kopf und **[44A]** _____ zu riskieren. Du magst diesen Sport sehr, nicht?

Phillip: Ja, darauf kannst du **[23D]** _____ nehmen! Es ist wirklich einfach. Du hast den **[34A]** _____ in **[24A]** _____raus. Die Sache hat nur einen **[22D]** _____ — wenn du über einen Stein fährst, kannst du plötzlich stolpern und fallen. Aber laß dich nicht entmutigen. Du mußt einfach bei der **[12A]** _____ bleiben, um besser zu werden. Oh, und wenn du mit jemandem zusammenstößt und dir einen Knochen brichst, gibt es eine Erstehilfehütte am Fuß des Berges. O.K., jetzt geht's um die **[1D]** _____! Einfach **[27A]** _____ drücken, daß du nicht aus Versehen über die Klippe fährst, wie ich letzte Woche. **[3D]** _____ und Beinbruch!

CROSSWORD PUZZLE

C. Match the columns.

☐ 1. Both tennis players are tied. The next game will determine the winner of the match. It's do or die!

☐ 2. When I heard footsteps in my house last night, my heart suddenly went into my throat.

☐ 3. I hear you have a job interview tomorrow. Break a leg!

☐ 4. The job offer is really good. There's only one hitch. I'd have to move to Greenland.

☐ 5. You're starting to play the guitar very well. If you stick to it, some day you'll be able to play like a pro!

☐ 6. Hans is a police officer. He risks life and limb every day.

☐ 7. I finally got the hang of changing a tire.

A. **Morgen werde ich meinen Chef um eine Gehaltserhöhung bitten. Drück mir ganz fest die Daumen!**

B. **Ich habe jetzt endlich den Bogen raus, wie man einen Reifen wechselt.**

C. **Du kannst schon einige Lieder auf der Gitarre spielen, und wenn du jetzt bei der Stange bleibst, spielst du bald wie ein Profi!**

D. **Mußt du so ein Spielverderber sein? Warum hast du die Musik ausgestellt? Wir hatten soviel Spaß beim Tanzen.**

E. **Hans ist ein Polizist. Er riskiert täglich Kopf und Kragen.**

F. **Das Jobangebot ist wirklich gut. Es hat nur einen Haken — Ich müßte nach Grönland ziehen.**

G. **Beide Tennisspieler halten denselben Punktestand. Das nächste Spiel bestimmt den Gewinner. Jetzt geht's um die Wurst!**

☐ 8. Do you have to be such a kill-joy? Why did you turn the music off? We were having so much fun dancing.

H. **"Willst du wirlich deinen Job kündigen?"**
"Darauf kannst du Gift nehmen! Ich kann meinen Chef nicht mehr ausstehen!"

☐ 9. "Are you going to quit your job?" "You better believe it! I can't tolerate my boss any longer!"

I. **Ich höre, du hast morgen ein Vorstellungsgespräch. Ich wünsche dir Hals und Beinbruch!**

☐ 10. Tomorrow I'm going to ask my boss for a raise. Keep your fingers crossed for me!

J. **Als ich letzte Nacht Schritte im Haus gehört habe ist mir das Herz total in die Hose gerutscht.**

D. DICTATION
Test Your Oral Comprehension

(This dictation can be found in Appendix A on page 174).

If you are following along with your cassette, you will now hear a series of sentences from the opening dialogue. These sentences will be read by a native speaker at normal conversational speed (which may seem fast to you at first). In addition, the words will be pronounced *as you would actually hear them in a conversation*, including many common reductions.

The first time the sentences are presented, simply listen in order to get accustomed to the speed and heavy use of reductions. The sentences will then be read again with a pause after each to give you time to write down what you heard. The third time the sentences are read, follow along with what you have written.

"mit allen Wassern gewaschen sein"

(trans): to know all the tricks of the trade
(lit): to be washed with all waters.

Dialogue in slang

Im Einkaufszentrum

Antje: Ich will ja nicht schon wieder **meinen Senf dazugeben**, aber mit der Verkäuferin hast du ja **nicht viel Federlesens gemacht**. Warum nur?

Christina: Sie hat mir erzählen wollen, daß das Kleid, das ich mir angesehen habe, ein Original sei. Dabei konnte ich sofort erkennen, daß es nur eine billige Imitation war. Die Frau **ist mit allen Wassern gewaschen**. Ich **nenne das Kind beim Namen**, und wenn sie denkt, sie kann mich **übers Ohr hauen, ist sie auf dem Holzweg**! Deshalb habe ich gleich erst einmal **andere Seiten aufgezogen**.

Antje: Ich weiß was du meinst. Manche Verkäufer **gehen über Leichen**, damit du was von ihnen kaufst. Sie lügen dir **das Blaue vom Himmel herunter**. Glaube mir, **ich kann ein Lied davon singen**.

Christina: Tja, jedenfalls **werfe ich mein Geld nicht zum Fenster heraus**. Oh, guck mal! Da ist ja diese automatische silberne Pizza-Schneidemaschine für DM300, nach der ich so lange gesucht habe!

Lesson Eight

Translation of dialogue

Antje: I don't mean **to butt in**, but you were **so short** with that saleswoman. How come?

Christina: She said that the dress I was looking at was an original, but I could tell that it was a cheap imitation. That woman is a **smooth operator**. I'm **calling a spade a spade**. If she thinks she can **pull the wool over my eyes**, she's **barking up the wrong tree**! That's why I decided **to get tough with her**.

Antje: I know what you mean. Some sales people will **stop at nothing** to get you to buy from them. They'll lie right to your face. Believe me, I can **go on and on about it**.

Christina: Well, you'll never see me **pouring my money down the drain**. Oh, look! There's that 300-mark automatic silver pizza-cutting machine I've been looking for!

Literal translation of dialogue

At the Mall

Antje: I don't mean **to add my mustard**, but you didn't **do much feather plucking** with that sales woman.

Christina: She said that the dress I was looking at was an original but I could tell that it was a cheap imitation. That woman is **washed with all the waters**. I'm **calling the child by its name**. If she thinks she can **hit me over the ear** than **she's on the woodway**! That's why I **put on a different set of strings** right away.

Antje: I know what you mean. Some sales people will **walk over corpses** to get you to buy from them. They'll **lie the blue out of the sky**. Believe me, I can **sing a song about it**.

Christina: Well, you'll never see me **tossing my money out the window**. Oh, look! There's that 300-mark automatic silver pizza-cutting machine I've been looking for!

Vocabulary

Blaue vom Himmel herunter lügen (das) *exp.* to lie constantly • (lit); to lie the blue out of the sky.

> usage example: Marie hat dir erzählt, daß sie in einem Film mitspielt? Glaub ihr bloß nicht. Sie lügt doch **das Blaue vom Himmel herunter**!

> translation: Marie told you that she's starring in a movie? Don't believe her. She lies about everything!

> literal translation: Marie told you that she's starring in a movie? Don't believe her. She lies the blue out of the sky!

OTHER IDIOMS USING "HIMMEL":

"Himmel, Arsch und Zwirn!" *exclam.* "Damn it!" • (lit): "Heaven, ass and twisted yarn!"

"Um Himmels Willen!" *exclam.* "For heaven's sake!" • (lit); "At heaven's will!"

freiem Himmel (unter) *exp.* outdoors • (lit); under free skies.

heiterem Himmel (aus) *exp.* out of the blue • (lit); out of the jolly sky.

Himmel und Hölle in Bewegung setzen *exp.* to accomplish something, to move heaven and earth • (lit); to get heaven and hell moving.

siebten Himmel sein/sich [wie] im siebten Himmel fühlen (im) *exp.* to be in seventh heaven • (lit); to be in the seventh heaven/to feel [like] being in the seventh heaven.

stinkt zum Himmel (etwas) *exp.* said of something that stinks to high heaven • (lit); something stinks to the sky/heaven.

Federlesens machen (nicht viel) *exp.* not to miss a beat (in doing something), without hesitation • (lit); not to pick off many feathers.

usage example: Die Firma machte **nicht viel Federlesens** und feuerte Georg sofort, als er beim Stehlen erwischt wurde.

translation: The company didn't miss a beat and fired George right away when he was caught stealing.

literal translation: The company didn't pick off many feathers and fired George right away when he was caught stealing.

Geld zum Fenster herauswerfen (das) *exp.* to waste one's money • (lit); to throw one's money out the window.

usage example: Diese Lederjacke ist viel zu teuer, so kann ich mein **Geld auch nicht zum Fenster hinauswerfen**.

translation: That leather jacket is much too expensive. I can't throw my money away like that.

literal translation: That leather jacket is much too expensive. I can't throw my money out of the window like that.

OTHER IDIOMS USING "GELD":

SEE: *page 92.*

Holzweg sein (auf dem) *exp.* to be very mistaken • (lit); to be on the wood way.

usage example: Wenn du denkst, daß ich dir noch einmal Geld leihen werde, bist du aber **auf dem Holzweg**.

translation: If you think I'd ever loan you money again, you're very mistaken.

literal translation: If you think I'd ever loan you money again, you're on the wood way.

Kind beim Namen nennen (das) *exp.* to call a spade a spade • (lit); to call the child by its name.

usage example: O.K. wenn ich **das Kind beim Namen nennen** soll, deine Schwester geht mit einem Schwachkopf aus!

translation: O.K. If I have to call a spade a spade, your sister is going out with a moron!

literal translation: O.K. If I have to call the child by its name, your sister is going out with a weak-head!

NOTE: **Schwachkopf** n. imbecile, moron • (lit); weak-head.

OTHER IDIOMS USING "KIND":

Kind mit dem Badewasser ausschütten (das) exp. to throw the baby out with the bath-water • (lit); to pour the baby out with the bath.

unschuldig wie ein neugeborenes Kind sein exp. to be as innocent as a new-born baby • (lit); to be as innocent as a new-born child.

Leichen gehen (über) exp. to be unscrupulous • (lit); to walk over corpses (to reach one's goal).

usage example: Er hat wirklich kein Gewissen. Er würde **über Leichen gehen**, nur um sein Ziel zu erreichen.

translation: He's got no conscience whatsoever. He would do absolutely anything to reach his goal.

literal translation: He's got no conscience whatsoever. He would walk over corpses to reach his goal.

Lied davon singen können (ein) exp. to know a lot about (something) • (lit); to be able to sing a song about (something).

usage example: Eine Grundschulklasse zu unterrichten ist nicht einfach. **Davon kann** ich, als Lehrerin, ein **Lied singen**.

translation: Teaching a class of first graders isn't easy. As a teacher, I know all about it

literal translation: Teaching a class of first graders isn't easy. As a teacher, I can sing a song about it.

Ohr hauen (jemanden über das) *exp.* to take advantage of someone • (lit); to hit someone over the ear.

usage example: Der Gebrauchtwagenhändler hat dich wirklich **übers Ohr gehauen**. Kein Auto ist $100.000 wert!

translation: That used car salesman really took advantage of you. No car is worth $100,000!

literal translation: That used car salesman really hit you over the ear. No car is worth $100,000!

OTHER IDIOMS USING "OHR":

SEE: *page 94.*

Saiten aufziehen (andere) *exp.* to come down on someone, to get tough with someone • (lit); to put on a different set of strings.

usage example: Wenn Klaus sich nicht bald daran gewöhnt, sein Zimmer aufzuräumen, werden seine Eltern **andere Saiten aufziehen** müssen.

translation: If Klaus doesn't get into the habit of cleaning his room soon, his parents will have to get tough with him.

literal translation: If Klaus doesn't get into the habit of cleaning his room soon, his parents will have to put on a different set of strings.

Senf dazugeben (seinen) *exp.* to add one's two cents • (lit); to add one's mustard.

usage example: Auf der Party mußte Barbara zu jeder Angelegenheit ihren **Senf dazugeben**.

translation: At the party Barbara had to add her two cents to every topic.

literal translation: At the party Barbara had to add her mustard to every topic.

Wassern gewaschen sein (mit allen) *exp.* to know all the tricks of the trade • (lit); to be washed with all the waters.

  usage example: Mein Steuerberater **ist mit allen Wassern gewaschen**. Er kann dir bestimmt mit deinem Steuerproblem helfen.

  translation: My accountant knows all the tricks of the trade. He can certainly help you with your tax problem.

  literal translation: My accountant is washed with all the waters. He can certainly help you with your tax problem.

OTHER IDIOMS USING "WASSER":

Schlag ins Wasser (ein) *exp.* • SEE: *p. 137.*

stille Wasser gründen tief *exp.* still waters run deep • (lit); silent waters are grounded deeply.

Wasser abgraben (jemandem) (das) *exp.* to pull the carpet from under someone's feet • (lit); to dig someone's water off.

Wasser fallen (ins) *exp.* to fall through • (lit); to fall in the water.

Wasser halten (sich über) *exp.* to keep one's head above water • (lit); to keep oneself above water.

Wasser reichen können (jemandem nicht das) *exp.* not to be able to hold a candle to someone • (lit); not to be able to pass the water to someone.

Practice The Vocabulary

(Answers to Lesson 8, p. 170)

A. Circle the corresponding letter of the word that best completes the idiom.

1. Die Frau ist mit allen _____ gewaschen.
   a. **Bädern**   b. **Wassern**   c. **Duschen**

2. Manche Verkäufer gehen über _____ , damit du was von ihnen kaufst.
   a. **Steine**   b. **Leute**   c. **Leichen**

3. Jedenfalls werfe ich mein Geld nicht zum _____ hinaus.
   a. **Fenster**   b. **Auto**   c. **Haus**

4. Ich nenne das _____ beim Namen.
   a. **Mädchen**   b. **Tier**   c. **Kind**

5. Sie lügen dir das _____ vom Himmel herunter.
   a. **Grüne**   b. **Rote**   c. **Blaue**

6. Wenn du denkst, daß ich dir noch einmal Geld borge, bist du aber auf dem _____.
   a. **Holzweg**   b. **Pfad**   c. **Rasen**

7. Eine Grundschulklasse zu unterrichten ist nicht einfach. Davon kann ich, als Lehrerin, ein _____ singen
   a. **Gedicht**   b. **Bild**   c. **Lied**

8. Der Gebrauchtwagenhändler hat dich wirklich übers _____ gehauen!
   a. **Auge**   b. **Ohr**   c. **Haar**

B. FIND-A-WORD CUBE
Find the answers from Exercise B in the cube below.

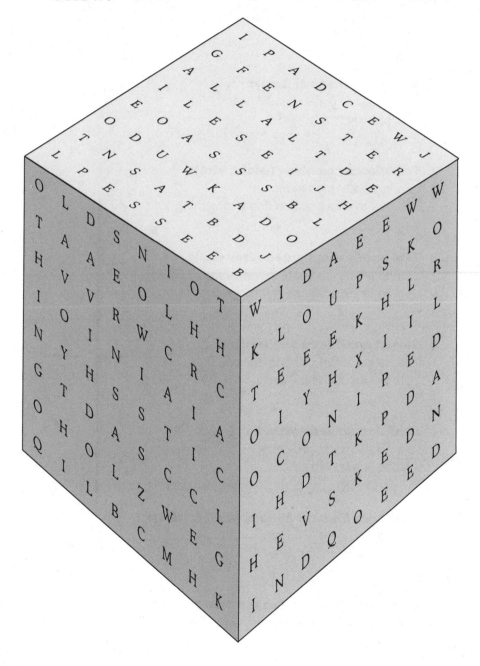

C. Choose the correct definition of the idiom.

1. **Blaue vom Himmel herunter lügen (das):**
   - ☐ a. to tell an outrageous lie
   - ☐ b. to tell an occasional lie

2. **Holzweg sein (auf dem):**
   - ☐ a. to call a spade a spade
   - ☐ b. to be very mistaken

3. **Federlesens machen (nicht viel):**
   - ☐ a. to waste one's money
   - ☐ b. not to miss a beat in doing something

4. **Ohr hauen (jemanden über das):**
   - ☐ a. to be able to relate to something
   - ☐ b. to take advantage of someone

5. **Saiten aufziehen (andere):**
   - ☐ a. to get tough with someone
   - ☐ b. to add one's two cents

6. **Senf dazugeben (seinen):**
   - ☐ a. to add one's two cents
   - ☐ b. to know all the tricks

7. **Geld zum Fenster hinauswerfen (das):**
   - ☐ a. to earn a lot of money
   - ☐ b. to waste one's money

8. **Kind beim Namen nennen (das):**
   - ☐ a. to call a spade a spade
   - ☐ b. to waste one's money

D. DICTATION
Test Your Oral Comprehension

(This dictation can be found in Appendix A on page 174).

If you are following along with your cassette, you will now hear a series of sentences from the opening dialogue. These sentences will be read by a native speaker at normal conversational speed (which may seem fast to you at first). In addition, the words will be pronounced *as you would actually hear them in a conversation,* including many common reductions.

The first time the sentences are presented, simply listen in order to get accustomed to the speed and heavy use of reductions. The sentences will then be read again with a pause after each to give you time to write down what you heard. The third time the sentences are read, follow along with what you have written.

sich Kopfzerbrechen bereiten

(trans): to worry someone
(lit): to cause oneself head breakage.

Dialogue in slang

Samstag Nacht

Achim: Würdest du heute Abend gern zum Essen und ins Kino ausgehen?

Sandra: Ich möchte schon, aber ich habe noch soviel Arbeit und morgen ist der Besitzer unserer Firma im Büro, daß heißt, das **dicke Ende kommt erst noch**. Ich sage dir, ich weiß nicht, **wo mir der Kopf steht**.

Achim: Ich will ja nicht meine **Nase in deine Angelegenheiten stecken** aber du solltest dir endlich mal **hinter die Ohren schreiben**, daß wenn du Tag und Nacht nur arbeitest, du davon noch einmal krank werden wirst. du mußt aber auch immer so einen **Dickschädel** haben! Ab und zu solltest du auch einmal so richtig **einen losmachen**. Ich muß dir sagen, daß du fängst an mir **Kopfzerbrechen zu bereiten**. Du lehnst meine Einladungen immer wegen deiner Arbeit ab.

Sandra: Du hast ja recht. Ich **komme dir auf halbem Weg entgegen**. Laß uns nach dem Abendessen treffen, und die neue Komödie mit dem französischen **Spinner** ansehen. Auf diese Weise kann ich noch etwas arbeiten bevor wir gehen. Ich muß zugeben, daß es ganz schön sein wird, mich mal wieder so richtig **totzulachen**. Selbst wenn es **ein Schlag ins Wasser** ist, wird mir etwas Spaß zur Abwechslung ganz gut tun. Oh, nur einen Gefallen: Kann ich deinen Laptop borgen und mitnehmen?

Lesson Nine

Translation 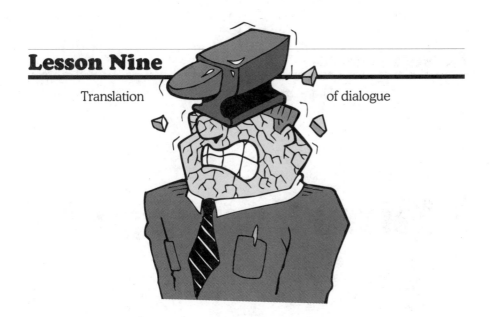 of dialogue

Achim: How would you like to go to dinner and the movies tonight?

Sandra: I'd like to, but I've got so much work to do; and tomorrow the owner of the company will be in the office which means that **the worst is yet to come**. I tell you, I don't know if I'm **coming or going**.

Achim: I don't mean **to poke my nose into your business**, but you've got **to get it into your head** that if you do nothing but work all day and night, you're going to make yourself sick. You're always so **stubborn** about this! You need **to live it up** once in a while. I have to tell you that you're starting **to worry me**. You always turn down my invitations because of work.

Sandra: All right. I'll **meet you halfway**. Let's get together after dinner and go see that new comedy with that French **wacko**. That way I can do some work before we go. I have to admit that it'll be nice **to laugh** again. Even if it's a **flop**, it'll do me good to do something fun for a change. Oh, one favor, can I borrow your laptop to take with us?

Literal translation of dialogue

Saturday Night

Achim: How would you like to go to dinner and the movies tonight?

Sandra: I'd like to, but I've got so much work to do and tomorrow the owner of the company will be in the office which means that **the thick end is still to come**. I tell you, I don't know **where my head's at**.

Achim: I don't mean **to poke my nose in your affairs**, but you've got **to write it behind your ears** that if you do nothing but work all day and night, you're going to make yourself sick. You always have to have such a **thick skull**! You need **to make one loose** every once in a while. I have to tell you that you're starting **to cause me head-cracking**. You always turn down my invitations because of work.

Sandra: All right. I'll **meet you halfway**. Let's get together after dinner and go see that new comedy with that french **wacko**. That way I can do some work before we go. I have to admit that it'll be nice **to laugh myself to death**. Even if it's a **hit in the water**, it'll do me good to do something fun for a change. Oh, one favor, can I borrow your laptop to take with us?

Vocabulary

Dickschädel haben (einen) *exp.* to be stubborn • (lit); to have a thick skull.

> usage example: Axel hat solch **einen Dickschädel**. Wenn er seinen Willen nicht kriegt, spricht er für Wochen nicht mit dir.
>
> translation: Axel is so stubborn. If he doesn't get his way, he won't talk to you for weeks.
>
> literal translation: Axel's got such a thick skull. If he doesn't get his way, he won't talk to you for weeks.

Ende kommt noch (das dicke) *exp.* the worst is yet to come • (lit); the thick end is still coming.

> usage example: Der Autounfall war noch nicht das schlimmste. **Das dicke Ende kommt** noch, wenn Karl vor Gericht muß.
>
> translation: The car accident wasn't the worst part. It's going to get worse when Karl has to appear in court.
>
> literal translation: The car accident wasn't the worst part. The thick end is still coming when Karl has to appear in court.

> OTHER IDIOMS USING "ENDE":
>
> > **Ende gehen (zu)** *exp.* to run out (of something) • (lit); to go to the end.
> >
> > **Ende gut, alles gut** *exp.* all's well that ends well • (lit); end good, all good.
> >
> > **Ende sein (am)** *exp.* to be at the end of one's patience (or power/abilities) • (lit); to be at the end.

falschen Ende anfassen (etwas am) *exp.* to go about something all wrong • (lit); to grasp something at the wrong end.

seinem Leben ein Ende machen/setzen (einer Sacher) *exp.* to put an end to something • (lit); to put/set an end to one's life/something.

halbem Wege entgegen kommen (jemandem auf) *exp.*
to compromise • (lit); to meet someone halfway.

usage example: Ich **komme dir auf halbem Wege entgegen**. Wenn du das Auto zu meinem Preis kaufst, gebe ich dir noch die Stereoanlage dazu.

translation: Let's compromise. If you buy the car at my asking price, I'll throw in the stereo.

literal translation: I'll meet you halfway. If you buy the car at my asking price, I'll throw in the stereo.

OTHER IDIOMS USING "WEG":

besten Weg sein, etwas zu tun (auf dem) *exp.* to be well on the way toward doing something • (lit); to be on the best way to do something.

neue Wege beschreiten/gehen *exp.* to break new ground • (lit); to tread/walk a new way.

schnellstem Weg(e) (auf) *exp.* as quickly as possible • (lit); on the fastest way.

Weg(e) gehen (jemandem aus dem) *exp.* to keep out of someone's way • (lit); to go out of someone's way.

Weg abkürzen (den) *exp.* to take a short cut • (lit); to shorten the way.

Weg abnehmen (jemandem einen) *exp.* to run an errand for someone • (lit); to take a way off someone.

Weg abschneiden (jemandem den) *exp.* to head someone off • (lit); to cut off someone's way.

Weg des geringsten Widerstands gehen (den) *exp.* to take the path of least resistance • (lit); to go the way of the least resistance.

Weg trauen (jemandem nicht über den) *exp.* not to trust someone at all • (lit); not to trust someone across the way.

Weg der Besserung sein (auf dem) *exp.* to be on the road to recovery • (lit); to be on the way of recovery.

Weg räumen (jemanden/etwas aus dem) *exp.* to get rid of someone/something • (lit); to clear something/someone out of the way.

Wege leiten (etwas in die) *exp.* to get something under way • (lit); to direct something on its way.

Kopfzerbrechen bereiten (sich) *exp.* to worry oneself • (lit); to cause oneself head breakage.

usage example: Manus Spielsucht bereitet mir langsam **Kopfzerbrechen**.

translation: Manu's gambling habit is starting to worry me.

literal translation: Manu's gambling habit is starting to cause me head breakage.

Kopf steht (nicht wissen, wo einem der) *exp.* not to know whether one is coming or going • (lit); not to know where one's head is.

usage example: Ich habe soviel Wäsche zu waschen, ich **weiß gar nicht, wo mir der Kopf steht**!

translation: I've got so much laundry to do, I don't know whether I'm coming or going!

literal translation: I've got so much laundry to do, I don't even know where my head is!

OTHER IDIOMS USING "KOPF":

SEE: *page 56.*

losmachen (einen) *exp.* to paint the town red • (lit); to make one loose.

> usage example: Heute Abend gehen wir alle zusammen aus. Da werden wir so richtig **einen losmachen**!
>
> translation: Tonight we're all going out together. We're really going to paint the town red!
>
> literal translation: Tonight we're all going out together. We're really going to untie one!

Nase in alles stecken (seine) *exp.* to be nosey • (lit); to put one's nose into everything.

> usage example: Ich kann meinen neuen Nachbarn nicht leiden. Er muß immer **seine Nase in alles stecken**.
>
> translation: I don't like my new neighbor. He's always so nosey.
>
> literal translation: I don't like my new neighbor. He always puts his nose into everything.

OTHER IDIOMS USING "NASE":

SEE: *page 42.*

Ohren schreiben (sich etwas hinter die) *exp.* to get something into one's (thick) head • (lit); to write something behind one's ears.

> usage example: Du mußt dir **hinter die Ohren schreiben**, den Ölstand in deinem Auto zu beachten, sonst ruinierst du noch den Motor.
>
> translation: You've got to get it into your head that you have to pay attention to the oil level in your car. If you don't, you're going to ruin the motor!

literal translation: You've got to write it behind your ears that you have to pay attention to the oil level in your car. If you don't, you're going to ruin the motor!

OTHER IDIOMS USING "OHR":

SEE: *page 94.*

Schlag ins Wasser (ein) *exp.* to be a complete flop • (lit); to be a hit in the water.

usage example: Die Büropartywar ein voller **Schlag ins Wasser**. Nur der Hausmeister kam!

translation: The office party was a compete flop. Only the janitor showed up!

literal translation: The office party was a hit in the water. Only the janitor showed up!

OTHER IDIOMS USING "SCHLAG":

keinen Schlag tun *exp.* not to do an ounce (of work) • (lit); not to do a stroke (of work).

Schlag (auf einen) *exp.* all at once • (lit); in one blow.

Schlag (weg)haben (einen) *exp.* to be crazy • (lit); to be a blow/hit short.

Schlag auf Schlag *exp.* in rapid succession • (lit); blow after blow [or] hit after hit.

Schlag ins Gesicht sein (ein) *exp.* to be a slap in the face • (lit); [same].

Schlag versetzen (jemandem einen) *exp.* to deal someone a real blow • (lit); to give someone a stroke/blow/hit.

Schläge kriegen *exp.* to get a thrashing • (lit); to receive a beating.

vernichtenden Schlag gegen jemanden führen (einen) *exp.* to deal someone a crushing blow • (lit); [same].

OTHER IDIOMS USING "WASSER":

SEE: *page 123.*

Spinner *exp.* screwball • (lit); loon.

usage example: Karl ist ein totaler **Spinner**. Er gießt seinen Garten, obwohl es regnet.

translation: Karl's a total nut. He's watering his garden even though it's raining.

literal translation: Karl is a total loon. He's watering his garden even though it's raining.

totlachen (sich) *exp.* to laugh hard • (lit); to laugh oneself to death.

usage example: Über den Film könnte ich mich **totlachen**!

translation: I can't stop laughing over that movie!

literal translation: I could laugh myself to death over that movie!

OTHER IDIOMS USING "LACHEN":

da gibt es gar nichts zu lachen *exp.* it's no laughing matter • (lit); there's nothing to laugh about.

die Sonne lacht *exp.* the sun is shining brightly • (lit); the sun is laughing.

platzen/sterben vor Lachen *exp.* to split one's sides laughing • (lit); to burst/die of laughter.

wer zuletzt lacht, lacht am besten *exp.* he who laughs last, laughs longest • (lit); he who laughs last, laughs best.

Practice The Vocabulary

(Answers to Lesson 9, p. 171)

A. Choose the definition that goes with the idiom.

A. to worry

B. not to know whether one is coming or going

C. to get something into one's (thick) head

D. to laugh hard

E. screwball

F. to paint the town red

G. to be a complete flop

H. to be stubborn

I. the worst is yet to come

J. to compromise

☐ 1. **Kopfzerbrechen bereiten (sich)** *exp.*

☐ 2. **Ende kommt noch (das dicke)** *exp.*

☐ 3. **Dickschädel haben (einen)** *exp.*

☐ 4. **halbem Wege entgegen kommen (jemandem auf)** *exp.*

☐ 5. **Ohren schreiben (sich etwas hinter die)** *exp.*

☐ 6. **totlachen (sich)** *exp.*

☐ 7. **Schlag ins Wasser (ein)** *exp.*

☐ 8. **losmachen (einen)** *exp.*

☐ 9. **Spinner** *m.*

☐ 10. **Kopf steht (nicht wissen, wo einem der)** *exp.*

B. Choose the correct word that completes the idiom.

1. Der Autounfall war noch nicht das Schlimmste. Das dicke (**Elend, Leid, Ende**) kommt noch, wenn Karl vor Gericht muß.

2. Du mußt dir mal hinter die (**Ohren, Augen, Arme**) schreiben, den Ölstand in deinem Auto zu beachten, sonst ruinierst du noch den Motor!

3. Über den Film könnte ich mich tot (**schreien, lachen, husten**).

4. Die Büroparty war ein voller Schlag ins (**Meer, Bier, Wasser**). Nur der Hausmeister kam!

5. Heute Abend gehen wir alle zusammen aus. Da werden wir so richtig einen (**los, straff, schmal**) machen.

6. Ich komme dir auf halbem (**Weg, Pfad, Grund**) entgegen. Wenn du das Auto zu meinem Preis kaufst, gebe ich dir noch die Stereoanlage dazu.

7. Manus Spielsucht bereitet mir langsam (**Fuß, Kopf, Mund**) zerbrechen.

8. Ich habe soviel Wäsche zu waschen, ich weiß gar nicht, wo mir der (**Arm, Kopf, Bein**) steht!

9. Ich kann meinen neuen Nachbarn nicht leiden. Er muß immer seine (**Rüssel, Zunge, Nase**) in alles stecken.

C. Match the columns.

□ 1. I don't mean to poke my nose into your business.

□ 2. You've got to get it into your head that if you do nothing but work all day and night, you're going to make yourself sick.

□ 3. You're always so stubborn about this.

□ 4. You need to live it up once in a while.

□ 5. I have to tell you that you're starting to worry me.

□ 6. The worst is yet to come.

□ 7. I don't know if I'm coming or going.

□ 8. I'll meet you halfway.

□ 9. He's a total nut.

□ 10. The office party was a complete flop.

A. **Du mußt aber auch immer so einen Dickschädel haben.**

B. **Ich komme dir auf halbem Weg entgegen.**

C. **Die Büroparty war ein voller Schlag ins Wasser.**

D. **Du solltest dir endlich hinter die Ohren schreiben, daß wenn du Tag und Nacht nur arbeitest, du davon noch mal krank wirst.**

E. **Das dicke Ende kommt erst noch.**

F. **Ich will ja nicht meine Nase in deine Angelegenheiten stecken.**

G. **Ich muß dir sagen, daß du anfängst, mir Kopfzerbrechen zu bereiten.**

H. **Er ist ein totaler Spinner.**

I. **Du solltest ab und zu auch mal so richtig einen losmachen.**

J. **Ich weiß nicht, wo mir der Kopf steht.**

D. DICTATION 📼
Test Your Oral Comprehension

(This dictation can be found in Appendix A on page 174).

If you are following along with your cassette, you will now hear a series of sentences from the opening dialogue. These sentences will be read by a native speaker at normal conversational speed (which may seem fast to you at first). In addition, the words will be pronounced *as you would actually hear them in a conversation,* including many common reductions.

The first time the sentences are presented, simply listen in order to get accustomed to the speed and heavy use of reductions. The sentences will then be read again with a pause after each to give you time to write down what you heard. The third time the sentences are read, follow along with what you have written.

Pudel dastehen
(wie ein begossener)

(trans): to look depressed and pitiful.
(lit): to stand there like a watered poodle.

Dialogue in slang

Im Nachtclub

Andreas: Ey, Bernd! **Was gibt's**? Du **stehst ja da wie ein begossener Pudel**.

Bernd: Ich bin schon vier Stunden hier und habe nicht ein einziges Mädchen kennengelernt. Ich dachte schon, diese eine **Tante** komme auf mich zu, aber das war nur **blinder Alarm**. Sie wollte zu dem Typen hinter mir. Was stimmt nur nicht mit mir?

Andreas: Das kannst du dir doch **an allen fünf Fingern abzählen**. Ich werde dir mal **reinen Wein einschenken**, und ich **nehme dabei kein Blatt vor den Mund**. Frauen **geben dir ständig einen Korb**, weil du immer nur auf deinem alten Thema **rumreitest**…Versicherungen. Ich weiß, das ist dein Beruf, aber Frauen finden das einfach nicht interessant. **Das Ende vom Lied** ist dann jedesmal, daß sie sich langweilen und dir **den Laufpass geben**. Vielleicht solltest du dir ein Hobby zulegen, damit du etwas hast, worüber du dich unterhalten kannst.

Bernd: Ich gebe dir völlig Recht. Tatsache ist, ich habe gerade gestern erst ein neues Hobby angefangen. Ich sammele verschiedene Fliegenarten aus aller Welt!

Andreas: …So Bernd, wie geht das Versicherungsgeschäft so heutzutage?

Lesson Ten

Translation  of dialogue

Andreas: Hey Bernd! **What's up**? You **look sad**.

Bernd: I've been here for four hours, and I haven't met a single girl. I thought this one **chick** was walking toward me, but it was a **false alarm**. She was walking up to the guy behind me. What's wrong with me?

Andreas: You can **predict** that this will happen. Listen, can we talk **privately**?

Bernd: Sure. Let's go to the back of the bar.

Andreas: **It's as plain as the nose on your face**. I'm going **to come clean with you**, and I'm not going to tell you this **in a roundabout way**. Women always **turn you down** because you keep **talking about the same old thing**... insurance. I know that's your profession, but women don't find that very interesting. The **upshot** is that they get bored and **dump** you. Maybe you should get a hobby. It would give you something else to talk about.

Bernd: I totally agree. In fact, just yesterday I started a new hobby. I'm collecting different species of flies from around the world!

Andreas: ...So Bernd. How is the insurance business going these days?

Literal translation of dialogue

At the Nightclub

Andreas: Hey Bernd! **What gives**? You look **like a poodle dog somebody poured water on**.

Bernd: I've been here four hours and I haven't met a single **aunt**. I thought this one **aunt** was walking toward me but it was a **false alarm**. She was walking up to the guy behind me. What's wrong with me?

Andreas: You can **count that off on all five fingers**. Listen, can we talk **under four eyes**?

Bernd: Sure. Let's go to the back of the bar.

Andreas: Okay, I'm gonna **pour you pure wine**, and I'm not **going to take a leaf in front of my mouth**. Women always **give you a basket** because **you keep riding** the same old theme…insurance. I know that's your profession, but women don't find that very interesting. The **end of the song** is that they get bored and **give you the running pass**. Maybe you should get a hobby. It would give you something else to talk about.

Bernd: I totally agree. In fact, just yesterday I started a new hobby. I'm collecting different species of flies from around the world!

Andreas: …So Bernd. How is the insurance business going these days?

Vocabulary

Alarm (blinder) *exp.* a false alarm • (lit); a blind alarm.

usage example: Wir dachten schon das Auto sei gestohlen worden, es war aber nur ein **blinder Alarm**. Opa hatte es in der falschen Straße geparkt.

translation: We thought the car had been stolen, but it was a false alarm. Grandpa parked it on the wrong street.

literal translation: We thought the car had been stolen, but it was a blind alarm. Grandpa parked it on the wrong street.

OTHER IDIOMS USING "ALARM":

Alarmzustand sein (im) *exp.* to be on alert, on stand-by • (lit); to be in a state of alarm.

Blatt vor den Mund nehmen (kein) *exp.* not to beat around the bush • (lit); to take a leaf in front of one's mouth.

usage example: Wenn du mit Gitte über ihr schlechtes Benehmen beim Abendessen sprichst, dann **nimm bloß kein Blatt vor den Mund**.

translation: When you talk to Gitte about her bad behavior at dinner, don't beat around the bush.

literal translation: When you talk to Gitte about her bad behavior at dinner, don't take a leaf in front of your mouth.

OTHER IDIOMS USING "BLATT":

anderen Blatt stehen (auf einem) *exp.* to be quite another matter • (lit); to stand on another leaf (or: written on another page).

OTHER IDIOMS USING "MUND":

SEE: *page 55.*

Ende vom Lied (das) *exp.* the outcome, the upshot • (lit); the end of the song.

> usage example: **Das Ende vom Lied** war, daß ich nach der Party alles allein aufräumen mußte.

> translation: The outcome was that after the party I had to clean up everything by myself.

> literal translation: The end of the song was that after the party I had to clean up everything by myself.

Fingern abzählen können (sich etwas an allen fünf)
exp. to be able to predict something • (lit); to be able to count something on all five fingers.

> usage example: Das hätte ich mir doch **an allen fünf Fingern abzählen** können, daß meine Mutter dieses Hotel nicht mögen würde.

> translation: I could have predicted that my mother wasn't going to like this hotel.

> literal translation: I could have counted off on all five fingers that my mother wasn't going to like this hotel.

> OTHER IDIOMS USING "FINGER":

SEE: *page 71.*

herumreiten (auf etwas) *exp.* to go on and on about the same subject • (lit); to ride about on something.

> usage example: Es ist wirklich schwer, sich mit Angela zu unterhalten. Sie **reitet** immer nur auf demselben Thema **herum**!

> translation: It's so hard talking to Angela. She always goes on and on about the same old thing!

> literal translation: It's so hard talking to Angela. She always rides about on the same theme!

> OTHER IDIOMS USING "REITEN":

> **"Hat Dich der Teufel geritten?"** *exp.* "Have you lost your mind?" • (lit); "Has the devil ridden you?"

Korb geben (jemandem einen) *exp.* to turn someone down • (lit); to give someone a basket.

usage example: Lotte hat Uwe schon wieder **einen Korb gegeben**. Heute ist einfach nicht sein Tag.

translation: Lotte turned Uwe down again. This is just not his night.

literal translation: Lotte gave Uwe a basket again. This is just not his night.

Pudel dastehen (wie ein begossener) *exp.* to look depressed, pitiful • (lit); to stand there like a soaked poodle.

usage example: Ich weiß, du hast den Wein nicht mit Absicht verschüttet! Jetzt stehe nicht **da, wie ein begossener Pudel**. Wir holen eine andere Flasche aus dem Keller.

translation: I know you didn't spill the wine on purpose! Don't stand there looking so depressed. We'll get another bottle from the cellar.

literal translation: I know you didn't spill the wine on purpose! Don't stand there like a soaked poodle. We'll get another bottle from the cellar.

Tante *exp.* (derogatory) woman/girl, chick • (lit); aunt.

usage example: Die **Tante** an der Abendkasse hat mir falsches Wechselgeld herausgegeben!

translation: That chick at the box office didn't give me enough change back!

literal translation: That aunt at the box office didn't give me the correct change!

"Was gibt's?" *exp.* "What's happening?" • (lit); "What gives?"

usage example: **Was gibt's**? Lange nicht gesehen!

translation: What's up? Long time no see!

literal translation: What gives? Long time no see!

OTHER IDIOMS USING "GEBEN":

da gibt's nichts *exp.* there's no doubt about it • (lit); there's nothing.

Fest geben (ein) *exp.* to throw a party • (lit); to give a feast.

ganze Liebe geben (jemandem seine) *exp.* to give someone all one's love • (lit); to give someone all of one's love.

geben (es sich) *exp.* • **1.** to get drunk • **2.** to put someone down • **3.** to beat oneself up (over something) • (lit); to give it to oneself.

geben (etwas von sich) *exp.* to utter something • (lit); to give something of oneself.

Hand geben (etwas [nicht] aus der) *exp.* not to let go of something • (lit); [not] to give something out of the hand.

Hand geben (jemandem die) *exp.* to shake someone's hand • (lit); to give someone the hand.

Hand geben (jemandem etwas in die) *exp.* to give someone something • (lit); to give someone something in the hand.

keinen Laut/Ton von sich geben *exp.* not to make a sound • (lit); not to give a sound/tone.

Reparatur geben (etwas in) *exp.* to take something in to be repaired • (lit); to give something to repair.

übergeben (sich) *exp.* to throw up • (lit); to overgive

was gibt es Neues? *exp.* what's new? • (lit); what gives it new?

wer gibt? *exp.* whose deal is it? (cards) / whose serve is it? (sports) • (lit); who gives?

Wort gab das andere (ein) *exp.* one word led to another • (lit); one word gave the other.

Wein einschenken (jemandem reinen) *exp.* to give it to someone straight • (lit); to pour someone pure wine.

usage example: Jemand muß Franz endlich **reinen Wein einschenken**, und ihm sagen, daß er gekündigt ist.

translation: Someone's finally got to give it to Franz straight and tell him he's fired.

literal translation: Someone has to pour Franz pure wine and tell him he's fired.

Practice The Vocabulary

(Answers to Lesson 10, p. 171)

A. Choose the correct definition of the idiom.

1. **Blatt vor den Mund nehmen (kein):**
   ☐ a. not to beat around the bush
   ☐ b. not to be able to predict something

2. **Pudel dastehen (wie ein begossener):**
   ☐ a. to turn someone down
   ☐ b. to look depressed

3. **herumreiten (auf etwas):**
   ☐ a. to go on and on about the same subject
   ☐ b. to turn someone down

4. **Tante:**
   ☐ a. fool, idiot
   ☐ b. woman/girl

5. **"Was gibt's?":**
   ☐ a. "Who gave you that?"
   ☐ b. "What's up?"

6. **Wein einschenken (jemandem reinen):**
   ☐ a. to beat up someone
   ☐ b. to give it to someone straight

7. **Ende vom Lied (das):**
   ☐ a. the outcome, the upshot
   ☐ b. a false alarm

8. **Fingern abzählen können (sich etwas an allen fünf):**
   ☐ a. to beat around the bush
   ☐ b. to be able to predict something

B. Choose the word that completes the idiom.

Alarm	gibt	Lied	Pudel	Tante
Fingern	Korb	Mund	reitet	Wein

1. Wir dachten schon, das Auto sei gestohlen worden, es war aber nur ein blinder _____ .

2. Wenn du mit Gitte über ihr schlechtes Benehmen beim Abendessen sprichst, dann nimm bloß kein Blatt vor den _____ .

3. Es ist wirklich schwer, sich mit Angela zu unterhalten. Sie _____ immer nur auf demselben Thema herum!

4. Lotte hat Uwe schon wieder einen _____ gegeben. Heute ist einfach nicht sein Tag.

5. Ich weiß, du hast den Wein nicht mit Absicht verschüttet! Jetzt stehe nicht da wie ein begossener _____ . Wir holen eine andere Flasche aus dem Keller.

6. Das Ende vom _____ war, daß ich nach der Party alles allein aufräumen mußte.

7. Das hätte ich mir doch an allen fünf _____ abzählen können, daß meine Mutter dieses Hotel nicht mögen würde.

8. Jemand muß Franz endlich reinen _____ einschenken und ihm sagen, daß er gekündigt ist.

9. Die _____ an der Abendkasse hat mir falsches Wechselgeld rausgegeben!

10. Was _____'s? Lange nicht gesehen!

FIND-A-WORD SPHERE

C. Using the list from exercise B, find and circle the words in the sphere below.

D. DICTATION

Test Your Oral Comprehension

(This dictation can be found in Appendix A on page 174).

If you are following along with your cassette, you will now hear a series of sentences from the opening dialogue. These sentences will be read by a native speaker at normal conversational speed (which may seem fast to you at first). In addition, the words will be pronounced *as you would actually hear them in a conversation*, including many common reductions.

The first time the sentences are presented, simply listen in order to get accustomed to the speed and heavy use of reductions. The sentences will then be read again with a pause after each to give you time to write down what you heard. The third time the sentences are read, follow along with what you have written.

REVIEW EXAM FOR LESSONS 6-10

(Answers to Review, p. 173)

A. MATCH THE COLUMNS
Choose the correct translation of the phrase in the right column.

☐ 1. In any case, you don't see me pouring my money down the drain.

☐ 2. I'm flabbergasted!

☐ 3. You look sad.

☐ 4. What's up?

☐ 5. That woman is a smooth operator.

☐ 6. I'll meet you halfway.

☐ 7. I don't know if I'm coming or going.

☐ 8. The weather today is just too good to be true.

☐ 9. That really didn't work out.

☐ 10. You bet your life!

A. **Was gibt's?**

B. **Ich komme dir auf halbem Weg entgegen.**

C. **Du stehst ja da wie ein begossener Pudel.**

D. **Darauf kannst du Gift nehmen!**

E. **Das Wetter heute ist einfach zu schön, um wahr zu sein.**

F. **Da bleibt mir ja die Spucke weg!**

G. **Jedenfalls werfe ich mein Geld nicht zum Fenster heraus.**

H. **Die Frau ist mit allen Wassern gewaschen.**

I. **Das ist ja wirklich in die Hose gegangen.**

J. **Ich weiß nicht, wo mir der Kopf steht.**

B. CROSSWORD

Step 1: **Fill in the blanks with the appropriate word(s) from the list below.**

Step 2: **Using your answers, fill in the crossword puzzle on page 159.**

BEINBRUCH	**HALS**	**NASE**
BLATT	**HEU**	**OHREN**
BOGEN	**HIMMEL**	**SCHLAG**
DAUMEN	**KIRCHENMAUS**	**SPUCKE**
DICKSCHÄDEL	**KOPFZERBRECHEN**	**STANGE**
DRAHT	**KORB**	**WASSERN**
ENDE	**KORN**	**WEIN**
FEDERLESENS	**KRAGEN**	**WURST**
FINGERN	**LEICHEN**	
HAKEN	**NAMEN**	

Across

1. **Da bleibt mir ja die** _____ **weg** *exp.* to be speechless.

17. _____ **kriegen (etwas in den falschen)** *exp.* to take something the wrong way

18. _____ **sein (auf)** *exp.* to be on one's toes.

22. **arm wie eine** _____ **sein** *exp.* to be dirt poor.

31. _____ **machen (nicht viel)** *exp.* not to miss a beat (in doing something), without hesitation.

38. _____ **vom Lied (das)** _exp._ the outcome, the upshot.

45. _____ **vor den Mund nehmen (kein)** _exp._ not to beat around the bush.

46. **Hals und** _____ **wünschen (jemandem)** _exp._ to wish someone good luck.

52. **Flinte nicht ins** _____ **werfen (die)** _exp._ not to throw in the towel.

60. **Blaue vom** _____ **herunter lügen (das)** _exp._ to lie constantly.

63. _____ **gewaschen sein (mit allen)** _exp._ to know all the tricks of the trade.

64. **Kind beim** _____ **nennen (das)** _exp._ to call a spade a spade.

72. _____ **gehen (über)** _exp._ to be unscrupulous.

75. _____ **abzählen können (sich etwas an allen fünf)** _exp._ to be able to predict something.

83. _____ **einschenken (jemandem reinen)** _exp._ to give it to someone straight.

Down

4. **Kopf und _____ riskieren** *exp.* to risk life and limb.

14. **_____ bleiben (bei der)** *exp.* to stick to doing something.

16. **_____ geben (jemandem einen)** *exp.* to turn someone down.

18. **_____ drücken (jemandem die)** *exp.* to keep one's fingers crossed for someone.

22. **_____ bereiten (sich)** *exp.* to worry someone.

29. **Geld wie _____ haben** *exp.* to be rich.

33. **_____ ins Wasser (ein)** *exp.* to be a complete flop.

39. **_____ schreiben (sich etwas hinter die)** *exp.* to get something into one's (thick) head.

40. **_____ haben (einen)** *exp.* to be stubborn.

51. **_____ raushaben (den)** *exp.* to get the hang of something.

54. **es geht um die _____** *exp.* to be do or die, now or never.

65. **_____ in alles stecken (seine)** *exp.* to be nosey.

74. **die Sache hat einen _____** *exp.* there's one hitch.

CROSSWORD PUZZLE

C. Underline the word that best completes the phrase.

1. Seeligman ist befördert worden?! Da bleibt mir ja die _____ weg!
   a. **Spucke**   b. **Schweiß**   c. **Wasser**

2. Du darfst einfach die Flinte nicht ins _____ werfen. Irgendwann
   schaffst du die Führerscheinprüfung schon.
   a. **Haus**   b. **Grüne**   c. **Korn**

3. Meine Zeichnung für den Kunstunterricht ist völlig in die _____
   gegangen. Es sollte ein Mädchen sein, sieht aber aus wie eine Birne.
   a. **Kleider**   b. **Hose**   c. **Röcke**

4. Heute Abend gehen wir alle zusammen aus. Da werden wir so
   richtig einen _____machen!
   a. **straff**   b. **groß**   c. **los**

5. Der Gebrauchtwagenhändler hat dich wirklich übers _____
   gehauen. Kein Auto ist $100.000 wert!
   a. **Auge**   b. **Haar**   c. **Ohr**

6. Das hätte ich mir doch an allen fünf _____ abzählen können, daß
   meine Mutter dieses Hotel nicht mögen würde.
   a. **Fingern**   b. **Zehen**   c. **Händen**

7. Ich kann meinen neuen Nachbarn nicht leiden. Er muß immer
   seine _____ in Alles stecken.
   a. **Ohren**   b. **Zunge**   c. **Nase**

8. Wenn du mit Gitte über ihr schlechtes Benehmen beim Abendessen
   sprichst, dann nimm bloß kein Blatt vor den _____.
   a. **Arm**   b. **Mund**   c. **Kopf**

9. Auf der Party mußte Barbara zu jeder Angelegenheit ihren _____ dazugeben.
   a. **Ketchup**   b. **Pfeffer**   c. **Senf**

10. Wir dachten schon, das Auto sei gestohlen worden, es war aber nur ein _____ Alarm. Opa hat es an der falschen Straße geparkt.
    a. **tauber**   b. **stummer**   c. **blinder**

11. Ich habe soviel Wäsche zu waschen, ich weiß gar nicht, wo mir der _____ steht!
    a. **Rücken**   b. **Kopf**   c. **Fuß**

12. Alle drei Tennisspieler halten denselben Punktestand. Das nächste Spiel bestimmt den Gewinner. Jetzt gehts um die _____!
    a. **Schinken**   b. **Salat**   c. **Wurst**

13. Lotte hat Uwe schon wieder einen _____ gegeben. Heute ist einfach nicht sein Tag.
    a. **Korb**   b. **Eimer**   c. **Trog**

14. Die Büroparty war ein voller Schlag ins _____. Nur der Hausmeister kam!
    a. **Bier**   b. **Wasser**   c. **Meer**

15. Der Autounfall war noch nicht das schlimmste. Das dicke _____ kommt erst noch, wenn Karl vor Gericht muß.
    a. **Ende**   b. **Elend**   c. **Leid**

16. Eine Grundschulklasse zu unterrichten ist nicht einfach. Davon kann ich, als Lehrerin, ein _____ singen.
    a. **Lied**   b. **Gedicht**   c. **Stück**

ANSWERS TO LESSONS 1-10 & REVIEW EXAMS

LEKTION EINS - *In der Schule (At School)*

Practice the Vocabulary

A. 1. Leber
   2. Hund
   3. Sand
   4. Westentasche

   5. Tode
   6. Nerven
   7. Leberwurst
   8. Seele

B. CROSSWORD

C. 1. B
   2. A
   3. C
   4. G
   5. D

   6. F
   7. H
   8. J
   9. E
   10. I

LEKTION ZWEI - *Auf der Party (At the Party)*
Practice the Vocabulary

A. 1. a.
   2. a
   3. b
   4. a
   5. b
   6. b

   7. b
   8. a
   9. b
   10. a
   11. a
   12. b

B. 1. F
   2. B
   3. D

   4. A
   5. C
   6. E

C. 1. c
   2. a
   3. c
   4. a

   5. c
   6. b
   7. a
   8. c

FIND-A-WORD PUZZLE

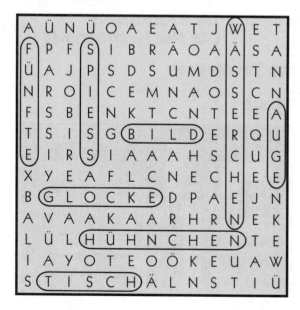

LEKTION DREI - *Der Hausgast* *(The House Guest)*

Practice the Vocabulary

A. 1. blau
   2. heißen
   3. Auge
   4. Arm

   5. Nase
   6. Ei
   7. Haut
   8. Teufel

B. 1. G
   2. B
   3. I
   4. C
   5. D

   6. A
   7. E
   8. F
   9. H

C. 1. J
   2. N
   3. H
   4. D
   5. B

   6. A
   7. L
   8. F
   9. E
   10. G

   11. M
   12. C
   13. K
   14. I

LEKTION VIER - *Im Restaurant* *(At the Restaurant)*

Practice the Vocabulary

A. **CROSSWORD**

B. 1. blasen
    2. links
    3. Ohren
    4. Kopf

    5. brechen
    6. grauen
    7. Auge
    8. Stein

C. 1. G
    2. F
    3. C
    4. A

    5. D
    6. B
    7. H
    8. E

LEKTION FÜNF - *Am Strand (At the Beach)*

Practice the Vocabulary

A. 1. b
    2. a
    3. b
    4. a
    5. a

    6. b
    7. a
    8. a
    9. a
    10. b

B. 1. a
    2. c
    3. c
    4. a

    5. c
    6. b
    7. a
    8. b

FIND-A-WORD PUZZLE

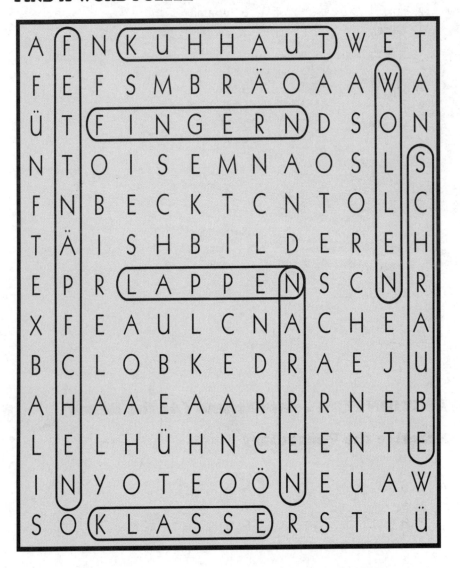

A	F	N	K	U	H	H	A	U	T	W	E	T
F	E	F	S	M	B	R	Ä	O	A	A	W	A
Ü	T	F	I	N	G	E	R	N	D	S	O	N
N	T	O	I	S	E	M	N	A	O	S	L	S
F	N	B	E	C	K	T	C	N	T	O	L	C
T	Ä	I	S	H	B	I	L	D	E	R	E	H
E	P	R	L	A	P	P	E	N	S	C	N	R
X	F	E	A	U	L	C	N	A	C	H	E	A
B	C	L	O	B	K	E	D	R	A	E	J	U
A	H	A	A	E	A	A	R	R	R	N	E	B
L	E	L	H	Ü	H	N	C	E	E	N	T	E
I	N	Y	O	T	E	O	Ö	N	E	U	A	W
S	O	K	L	A	S	S	E	R	S	T	I	Ü

C. 1. D   5. E
    2. F   6. A
    3. G   7. B
    4. C   8. H

REVIEW EXAM FOR LESSONS 1-5
Practice the Vocabulary

A. 1. ein Herz
    2. der Hund
    3. Augen
    4. Glocke

    5. Arm
    6. blau
    7. Kopf
    8. Ton

B. **CROSSWORD**

C. 1. a   6. a   11. b
   2. b   7. b   12. a
   3. b   8. a   13. a
   4. b   9. b   14. a
   5. b   10. a

LEKTION SECHS - *Im Supermarkt (At the Market)*

Practice the Vocabulary

A. 1. Hose   5. Ohren
   2. Spucke   6. Karte
   3. Draht   7. Kugel
   4. Heu   8. Nummer

B. **Find-a-Word Cube**

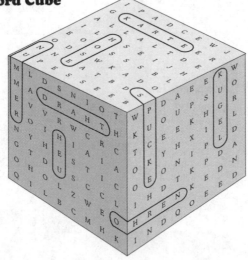

C. 1. E   6. B
   2. H   7. D
   3. C   8. J
   4. A   9. F
   5. G   10. I

LEKTION SIEBEN - *Ein Ski Ausflug (A Skiing Trip)*

Practice the Vocabulary

A. 1. Spitze
2. Hals
3. wahr
4. Wurst

5. Gift
6. Stange
7. Hose
8. Daumen

B. **CROSSWORD**

C. 1. G   6. E
    2. J   7. B
    3. I   8. D
    4. F   9. H
    5. C   10. A

LEKTION ACHT - *Im Einkaufszentrum (At the Mall)*

Practice the Vocabulary

A. 1. b   5. c
    2. c   6. a
    3. a   7. c
    4. c   8. b

B. **Find-a-Word Cube**

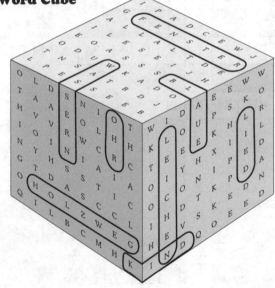

C. 1. a   5. a
    2. b   6. a
    3. b   7. b
    4. b   8. a

LEKTION NEUN - *Samstag Nacht (Saturday Night)*

Practice the Vocabulary

A. 1. A
   2. I
   3. H
   4. J
   5. C

6. D
7. G
8. F
9. E
10. B

B. 1. Ende
   2. Ohren
   3. lachen
   4. Wasser
   5. los

6. Weg
7. Kopf
8. Kopf
9. Nase

C. 1. F
   2. D
   3. A
   4. I
   5. G

6. E
7. J
8. B
9. H
10. C

LEKTION ZEHN - *Im Nachtclub (At the Nightclub)*

Practice the Vocabulary

A. 1. a
   2. b
   3. a
   4. b

5. b
6. b
7. a
8. b

B. 1. Alarm   6. Lied
    2. Mund   7. Fingern
    3. reitet   8. Wein
    4. Korb   9. Tante
    5. Pudel   10. gibt

C. **FIND-A-WORD SPHERE**

REVIEW EXAM FOR LESSONS 6-10
Practice the Vocabulary

A. 1. G   6. B
    2. F   7. J
    3. C   8. E
    4. A   9. I
    5. H   10. D

B. **CROSSWORD**

C. 1. a   7. c   13. a
    2. c   8. b   14. b
    3. b   9. c   15. a
    4. c   10. c   16. a
    5. c   11. b
    6. a   12. c

APPENDIX
-Dictation-

Lektion Eins

In der Schule (At School)

1. Was ist dir nur für eine **Laus über die Leber gelaufen**?
2. Warum **spielst du die beleidigte Leberwurst**?
3. Ich habe die Erdkundearbeit **in den Sand gesetzt**.
4. Da habe ich mir wirklich **einen groben Schnitzer** erlaubt!
5. Dabei dachte ich, ich kenne Europa **wie meine Westentasche**.
6. Das hat mich wirklich **aus der Fassung gebracht**.
7. Erdkunde **langweilt mich zu Tode**.
8. Frau Rater **geht mir so auf die Nerven**.

Lektion Zwei

Auf der Party (At the Party)

1. Ich fühle mich wie **das fünfte Rad am Wagen**.
2. Alle sind so **aufgetakelt**.
3. Das ist ja **ein Bild für die Götter**!
4. Mit ihr **habe ich auch noch ein Hühnchen zu rupfen**.
5. Ich habe ihr was **unter vier Augen** anvertraut.
6. Jetzt **drehe ich den Spieß um**.
7. Der werde ich **die Leviten lesen**!
8. Sie sieht aus als **könnte sie kein Wässerchen trüben**.

Lektion Drei

Der Hausgast (The House Guest)

1. Ich könnte mich **grün und blau ärgern**.
2. Er ist ein **Schmuddel wie er im Buche steht**.
3. Ich **habe so die Nase von ihm voll**.
4. Unser Haus war immer **wie aus dem Ei gepellt**.
5. Du scheinst ja wirklich **mit deinem Latein am Ende** zu sein.
6. Ich bin ja richtig froh, daß ich **nicht in deiner Haut stecke**.
7. **Du nimmst mich doch auf den Arm**!
8. Du mußt aufhören, **um den heißen Brei zu reden**.

Lektion Vier

Im Restaurant (At the Restaurant)

1. Ich **hatte heute soviel um die Ohren** bei der Arbeit.
2. Die scheint ja ständig **einen Streit vom Zaun zu brechen**.
3. Du mußt wirklich lernen, nicht jedes ihrer **Worte auf die Goldwaage zu legen**.
4. Ich muß ihr wirklich **ein Dorn im Auge sein**.
5. Sie hat mich die ganze Woche lang ohne Grund **links liegen lassen**, dabei ist sie doch sonst **nicht auf den Mund gefallen**.
6. Da hast du **den Nagel auf den Kopf getroffen**.
7. **Ich lasse mir darüber keine grauen Haare wachsen**.
8. Wenn sie sich dann **im Ton vergreift** werde ich ihr gehörig **den Marsch blasen**!

Lektion Fünf

Am Strand (At the Beach)

1. Er **paßt mir immer noch wie angegossen**.
2. Ist sie **von allen guten Geistern verlassen**?
3. **Bei ihr ist doch eine Schraube locker**.
4. Was sie sich immer so **aus den Fingern saugt, geht auf keine Kuhhaut**.
5. Du hättest sie zwingen sollen, **Farbe zu bekennen**.
6. Da ging dir eine Gelegenheit **durch die Lappen**.
7. Das wär doch was gewesen, sie so **ins Fettnäpfchen treten** zu sehen.

Lection Sechs

Im Supermarkt (At the Market)

1. Den einen Tag hat er **Geld wie Heu**, den anderen Tag ist er **arm wie eine Kirchenmaus**.
2. Warum mußte er auch **alles auf eine Karte setzen**?
3. Ich **gehe immer auf Nummer sicher**.
4. Das ist ja wirklich **in die Hose gegangen**.
5. Er **schiebt hier eine etwas ruhigere Kugel** als bei einer großen Bank.
6. Na, nach sowas kann man nur **die Ohren steif halten** und **darf die Flinte nicht ins Korn werfen**.

Lektion Sieben

Ein Skiausflug (A Skiing Trip)

1. Das Wetter heute ist einfach **zu schön, um wahr zu sein.**
2. Mir ist **das Herz total in die Hose gerutscht!**
3. Ich bin schon soweit **Kopf und Kragen zu riskieren.**
4. **Darauf kannst du Gift nehmen!**
5. Du **hast den Bogen** in **Nullkommanix raus.**
6. Du mußt einfach **bei der Stange bleiben,** um besser zu werden.
7. **Jetzt geht's um die Wurst!**
8. Einfach **Daumen drücken,** daß du nicht aus Versehen über die Klippe fährst!

Lektion Acht

Im Einkaufszentrum (At the Mall)

1. Mit der Verkäuferin hast du ja **nicht viel Federlesens gemacht.**
2. Die Frau **ist mit allen Wassern gewaschen.**
3. Ich **nenne das Kind beim Namen,** und wenn sie denkt, sie kann mich **übers Ohr hauen, ist sie auf dem Holzweg!**
4. Deshalb hatte ich gleich erstmal **andere Saiten aufgezogen.**
5. **Ich kann ein Lied davon singen.**
6. Tja, jedenfalls **werfe ich mein Geld nicht zum Fenster raus.**

Lektion Neun

Samstag Nacht (Saturday Night)

1. Das **dicke Ende kommt erst noch**.
2. Ich sage es dir, ich weiß nicht, **wo mir der Kopf steht**.
3. Ich will ja nicht meine **Nase in deine Angelegenheiten stecken**.
4. Du mußt aber auch immer so einen **Dickschädel** haben!
5. Du solltest ab und zu auch mal so richtig **einen los machen**.
6. Du fängst an, mir **Kopfzerbrechen zu bereiten**.
7. Ich **komme dir auf halbem Weg entgegen**.
8. Es wäre ganz schön, mich mal wieder so richtig **totzulachen**.

Lektion Zehn

Im Nachtclub (At the Nightclub)

1. **Was gibt's**?
2. Du **stehst ja da wie ein begossener Pudel**.
3. Ich dachte schon diese eine **Tante** kommt auf mich zu, aber das war nur **blinder Alarm**.
4. Das kannst du dir doch **an allen fünf Fingern abzählen**.
5. Ich werde dir mal **reinen Wein einschenken**, und ich **nehme dabei kein Blatt vor den Mund**.
6. Frauen **geben dir ständig einen Korb**, weil du immer nur auf deinem alten Thema **rumreitest**…Versicherungen.
7. **Das Ende vom Lied** ist dann jedesmal, daß sie sich langweilen und dir **den Laufpass geben**.

Glossary

Alarm (blinder) *exp.* a false alarm • (lit); a blind alarm.

usage example: Wir dachten schon das Auto sei gestohlen worden, es war aber nur ein **blinder Alarm**. Opa hatte es in der falschen Straße geparkt.

translation: We thought the car had been stolen, but it was a false alarm. Grandpa parked it on the wrong street.

literal translation: We thought the car had been stolen, but it was a blind alarm. Grandpa parked it on the wrong street.

OTHER IDIOMS USING "ALARM":

Alarmzustand sein (im) *exp.* to be on alert, on stand-by • (lit); to be in a state of alarm.

angegossen passen (wie) *exp.* to fit like a glove • (lit); to fit as if something were cast on.

usage example: Das Kleid ist genau die richtige Größe, es **paßt wie angegossen**!

translation: This dress is the perfect size. It fits like a glove!

literal translation: That dress is the perfect size. It fits as if it were cast on!

Arm nehmen (jemanden auf den) *exp.* to pull one's leg • (lit); to take someone up on one's arm.

usage example: Andrea geht dieses das Wochenende zelten? Du willst mich wohl **auf den Arm nehmen**. Sie hat doch Platzangst. Sie schläft doch niemals in einem Zelt!

translation: Andrea is going camping this weekend? You're pulling my leg. She's claustrophobic. She'll never sleep in a tent!

literal translation: Andrea is going camping this weekend? You want to take me up the arm. She's claustrophobic. She'll never sleep in a tent!

arm wie eine Kirchenmaus sein *exp.* to be dirt poor • (lit); to be as poor as a church mouse.

usage example: Es ist schwer zu glauben, daß Lydia mal **arm wie eine Kirchenmaus** war. Heute hat sie mehrere Geschäfte.

translation: It's hard to believe that Lydia used to be dirt poor. Today she owns several businesses.

literal translation: It's hard to believe that Lydia used to be as poor as a church mouse. Today she owns several businesses.

OTHER IDIOMS USING "ARM":

Arm in Arm gehen *exp.* to walk arm in arm • (lit); to go arm in arm.

Arme greifen (jemandem unter die) *exp.* to give someone a hand financially • (lit); to grab someone under the arms.

Arme laufen (jemandem in die) *exp.* to meet someone by chance • (lit); to walk into someone's arms.

offenen Armen empfangen (jemanden mit) *exp.* to receive someone with open arms • (lit); [same].

aufgetakelt sein *exp.* to get all dolled up • (lit); with all sails set.

usage example: Frau Schulze kam völlig **aufgetakelt** in die Kirche. Ihr Minirock und die hohen Schuhe waren wirklich unangemessen.

translation: Miss Schulze came to church all dolled up. Her miniskirt and those high heels were really inappropriate.

literal translation: Miss Schulze came to church with all sails set. Her miniskirt and those high heels were really inappropriate.

Auge zudrücken (ein) *exp.* to turn a blind eye • (lit); to squeeze one eye shut.

usage example: Der Verkehrspolizist hat nochmal **ein Auge zugedrückt** und mir keinen Strafzettel gegeben.

translation: The cop turned a blind eye and didn't give me a ticket.

literal translation: The cop squeezed one eye shut and didn't give me a ticket.

Augen sprechen (mit jemandem unter vier) *exp.* to speak privately with someone • (lit); to talk under four eyes.

usage example: Ich muß dir eine Geheimnis anvertrauen, können wir irgendwo **unter vier Augen sprechen**?

translation: I have to tell you a secret. Can we talk somewhere in private?

literal translation: I have to tell you a secret. Can we talk somewhere under four eyes?

OTHER IDIOMS USING "AUGE/AUGEN":

aller Augen (vor) *exp.* in front of everyone • (lit); before all eyes.

Auge behalten (etwas im) *exp.* to bear something in mind • (lit); to keep something in the eye.

Auge beleidigen (das) *exp.* to be an eyesore • (lit); to offend the eye.

Auge fassen (etwas ins) *exp.* to contemplate something • (lit); to seize something in the eye.

Auge geworfen haben (auf etwas ein) *exp.* to have one's sight set on something • (lit); to have thrown an eye on something.

Auge haben (etwas im) *exp.* to have one's eye on something • (lit); to have something in the eye.

Auge riskieren (ein) *exp.* to have a look • (lit); to risk an eye.

Auge stechen (ins) *exp.* to catch the eye • (lit); to stab in the eye.

Auge um Auge *exp.* an eye for an eye • (lit); eye for eye.

Auge zumachen (kein) *exp.* not to sleep a wink • (lit); not to close an eye.

Augen sehen (jemanden/etwas mit anderen) *exp.* to see someone/something in a different light • (lit); to see someone/something with different eyes.

Augen (in meinen) *exp.* in my opinion • (lit); in my eyes.

Augen an etwas weiden (die) *exp.* to feast one's eyes on • (lit); to graze the eyes on something.

Augen aus dem Kopf weinen (sich die) *exp.* to cry one's eyes out • (lit); to cry one's eyes out of the head.

Augen, aus dem Sinn (aus den) *exp.* out of sight, out of mind • (lit); out of the eyes, out of the mind.

Augen gesehen haben (etwas mit eigenen) *exp.* to have seen something with one's own eyes • (lit); [same]

Augen machen (große)
exp. to be wide-eyed • (lit);
to make big eyes.

**Augen offen
haben/offen halten
(die)** *exp.* to keep one's
eyes peeled • (lit); to
have/keep the eyes open.

**Augen öffnen
(jemandem die)** *exp.* to
open someone's eyes •
(lit); [same].

Augen schließen (die)
exp. to fall asleep • (lit); to
close the eyes.

**Augen sehen
(jemandem in die)** *exp.*
to look someone in the
eye(s) • (lit); to see
someone in the eye.

**Augen sind größer als
der Magen/Bauch
(die)** *exp.* to have eyes
bigger than one's stomach
• (lit); the eyes are bigger
than the stomach.

**Augen vor etwas
verschließen (die)** *exp.*
to close one's eyes to
something • (lit); to close
the eyes before something.

Augenblick *exp.* a
moment, blink of an eye •
(lit); [same].

Augenweide *exp.* pleasing
to the eye • (lit);
eye-grazing.

blauäugig *exp.* naive • (lit);
blue-eyed.

blaues Auge (ein) *exp.* a
black eye • (lit); a blue eye.

bloßen Auge (mit dem)
exp. with the naked eye •
(lit); with bare eyes.

**da muß man seine
Augen überall
(hinten und vorn)
haben** *exp.* you need eyes
in the back of your head •
(lit); one must have one's
eyes everywhere (or back
and front).

**geistigen Auge (vor
meinem)** *exp.* in my
mind's eye • (lit); before
my spiritual eye.

schöne Augen machen
exp. to flirt with someone •
(lit); to make pretty eyes.

**schöne/verliebte Augen
machen (jemandem)**
exp. to make eyes at
someone (lit); to make
beautiful/ loving eyes at
someone.

**sein Ziel im Auge
behalten** *exp.* to keep
one's goal in mind • (lit); to
keep one's goal in the eye.

**sicheres Auge für etwas
haben (ein)** *exp.* to have
a good eye for something •
(lit); to have a sure eye for
something.

soweit das Augen reicht
exp. as far as the eye can
see • (lit); as far as the eye
reaches.

B

**Bild für die Götter sein
(ein)** *exp.* to be a sight to
behold • (lit); to be a picture for
the gods.

usage example: Jochen hat den
ganzen Nachmittag in der
Schlammpfütze gespielt — **ein
Bild für die Götter**!

translation: Jochen played in a
mud puddle all afternoon. What
a sight to behold!

literal translation: Jochen played
in a mud puddle all afternoon. A
picture for the gods!

OTHER IDIOMS USING "BILD":

Bild machen (sich ein)
exp. to get the picture •
(lit); to make a picture for
oneself.

**Bild von einem
Mann/einer Frau
(ein)** *exp.* a picture
perfect man/woman • (lit);
a picture of a man/woman.

Bilde sein über (im) *exp.*
to be aware of something •
(lit); to be in the picture.

Kopf oder Zahl *exp.* heads
or tails • (lit); head or
number.

**Blatt vor den Mund
nehmen (kein)** *exp.* not to
beat around the bush • (lit); to
take a leaf in front of one's
mouth.

usage example: Wenn du mit
Gitte über ihr schlechtes
Benehmen beim Abendessen
sprichst, dann **nimm bloß
kein Blatt vor den Mund**.

translation: When you talk to
Gitte about her bad behavior at
dinner, don't beat around the
bush.

literal translation: When you talk
to Gitte about her bad behavior
at dinner, don't take a leaf in
front of your mouth.

OTHER IDIOMS USING "BLATT":

**anderen Blatt stehen
(auf einem)** *exp.* to be
quite another matter • (lit);
to stand on another leaf (or:
written on another page).

**Blaue vom Himmel
herunter lügen (das)** *exp.*
to lie constantly • (lit); to lie the
blue out of the sky.

usage example: Marie hat dir erzählt, daß sie in einem Film mitspielt? Glaub ihr bloß nicht. Sie lügt doch **das Blaue vom Himmel herunter**!

translation: Marie told you that she's starring in a movie? Don't believe her. She lies about everything!

literal translation: Marie told you that she's starring in a movie? Don't believe her. She lies the blue out of the sky!

OTHER IDIOMS USING "HIMMEL":

"Himmel, Arsch und Zwirn!" *exclam.* "Damn it!" • (lit): "Heaven, ass and twisted yarn!"

"Um Himmels Willen!" *exclam.* "For heaven's sake!" • (lit); "At heaven's will!"

freiem Himmel (unter) *exp.* outdoors • (lit); under free skies.

heiterem Himmel (aus) *exp.* out of the blue • (lit); out of the jolly sky.

Himmel und Hölle in Bewegung setzen *exp.* to accomplish something, to move heaven and earth • (lit); to get heaven and hell moving.

siebten Himmel sein/sich [wie] im siebten Himmel fühlen (im) *exp.* to be in seventh heaven • (lit); to be in the seventh heaven/to feel [like] being in the seventh heaven.

stinkt zum Himmel (etwas) *exp.* said of some-thing that stinks to high heaven • (lit); something stinks to the sky/heaven.

Bogen raushaben (den)

exp. to get the hang of something • (lit); to get the arch on something.

usage example: Ich habe jetzt endlich **den Bogen raus**, wie man einen Reifen wechselt.

translation: I finally got the hang of changing a tire.

literal translation: I finally got the curve on how to change a tire.

OTHER IDIOMS USING "BOGEN":

Bogen überspannen (den) *exp.* to go too far • (lit); to overstretch the bow.

großen Bogen um jemanden machen (einen) *exp.* to stay clear of someone • (lit); to make a big arc around someone.

breitschlagen lassen
(sich) *exp.* to let oneself be talked into doing something • (lit); to let oneself be pounded flat and wide.

usage example: Ich habe mich schon wieder zum Abwaschen **breitschlagen lassen**.

translation: I let myself be talked into doing the dishes again.

literal translation: I let myself be pounded flat and wide into doing the dishes again.

NOTE: The verb **breitschlagen** means "to pound something until it is flat and wide." (**breit** *adj.* wide • **schlagen** *exp.* to hit, pound, slap).

Buche steht (wie er/sie/es
im) *exp.* to be a textbook example of something • (lit); to be depicted in a book.

usage example: Marion ist eine Verkäuferin **wie sie im Buche steht**. Sie hat diese Woche dreimal mehr verkauft als ihre Mitarbeiterinnen.

translation: Marion is a textbook example of a salesperson. She sold three times as much this week as her co-workers.

literal translation: Marion is a salesperson as depicted in a book. She sold three times as much this week as her co-workers.

OTHER IDIOMS USING "BUCH/BUCHE":

Buchführung *exp.* to keep books (accounting) • (lit); to lead a book.

Büchern sitzen (über den) *exp.* to pore over one's books • (lit); to sit over the books.

wie ein Buch mit sieben Siegeln *exp.* incomprehensible • (lit); like a book with seven seals.

wie ein Buch reden *exp.* to talk like a book • (lit); [same].

Da bleibt mir ja die
Spucke weg *exp.* to be speechless • (lit); to be spitless.

usage example: Seeligman ist befördert worden?! **Da bleibt mir ja die Spucke weg**!

translation: Seeligman got a promotion?! I'm speechless!

literal translation: Seeligman got a promotion?! That leaves me spitless!

das geht auf keine Kuhhaut *exp.* to be beyond belief • (lit); it doesn't go on a cow hide.

usage example: Wie der mit seinem neuen Auto angibt, **geht auf keine Kuhhaut mehr**.

translation: The way he's bragging about his new car is really beyond belief.

literal translation: The way he's bragging about his new car won't fit on a cow hide.

Daumen drücken (jemandem die) *exp.* to keep one's fingers crossed for someone • (lit); to keep one's thumbs pressed for someone.

usage example: Morgen werde ich meinen Chef um eine Gehaltserhöhung bitten. **Drück mir ganz fest die Daumen**!

translation: Tomorrow I'm going to ask my boss for a raise. Keep your fingers crossed for me!

literal translation: Tomorrow I'm going to ask my boss for a raise. Please press your thumbs real hard for me!

OTHER IDIOMS USING "DAUMEN":

Daumen peilen (über den) *exp.* roughly, approximately • (lit); over the thumb.

Daumen drehen (die) *exp.* to twiddle one's thumbs • (lit); to turn the thumbs.

Daumen halten (jemanden) (unter dem) *exp.* to keep someone under one's thumb • (lit); [same].

Denkzettel verpassen (jemandem einen) *exp.* to teach someone a lesson • (lit); to issue someone a thinking note.

usage example: Mein kleiner Bruder hat schon wieder mein Auto geliehen ohne zu fragen. Diesmal werde ich ihm aber **einen Denkzettel verpassen**!

translation: My little brother borrowed my car again without asking. This time, I'm going to teach him a lesson!

literal translation: My little brother borrowed my car again without asking. This time, I'm going to issue him a thinking note!

Dickschädel haben (einen) *exp.* to be stubborn • (lit); to have a thick skull.

usage example: Axel hat solch **einen Dickschädel**. Wenn er seinen Willen nicht kriegt, spricht er für Wochen nicht mit dir.

translation: Axel is so stubborn. If he doesn't get his way, he won't talk to you for weeks.

literal translation: Axel's got such a thick skull. If he doesn't get his way, he won't talk to you for weeks.

die Sache hat einen Haken *exp.* there's one hitch • (lit); the matter has one hook.

usage example: Das Jobangebot ist wirklich gut. Es hat nur **einen Haken** — Ich müßte nach Grönland ziehen.

translation: The job offer is really good. There's only one hitch. I'd have to move to Greenland.

literal translation: The job offer is really good. It has only one hook. I'd have to move to Greenland.

Dorn im Auge sein (jemandem ein) *exp.* to be a thorn in one's side • (lit); to be a thorn in someone's eye.

usage example: Ich bin froh, daß wir endlich unser Haus streichen. Die alte Farbe war mir schon immer **ein Dorn im Auge**.

translation: I'm glad we're finally painting our house. The old color has always been a thorn in my side.

literal translation: I'm glad we're finally painting our house. The old color has always been a thorn in my eye.

Draht sein (auf) *exp.* to be on one's toes • (lit); to be on wire.

usage example: Als Feuerwehrmann muß man immer **auf Draht sein**.

translation: As a firefighter, you always have to be on your toes.

literal translation: As a firefighter, you always have to be on wire.

OTHER IDIOMS USING "DRAHT":

heißer Draht *exp.* hot line • (lit); hot wire.

Ei gepellt (wie aus dem) *exp.* to be as neat as a pin • (lit); like peeled from an egg.

usage example: Alle Schüler sahen auf der Abschlußfeier **wie aus dem Ei gepellt** aus, bis auf Hugo, der in Jeans und T-shirt kam.

translation: All the students looked immaculate at their graduation ceremony except for Hugo, who came in jeans and T-shirt.

literal translation: All the student looked peeled from an egg at their graduation ceremony except for Hugo, who came in jeans and T-shirt.

das Ei des Kolumbus *exp.* (said of something extremely simple yet not obvious) to be under one's nose the whole time • (lit); the egg of Columbus.

das sind ungelegte Eier! *exp.* We'll cross that bridge when we come to it! • (lit); these are unlaid eggs.

wie ein Ei dem andern gleichen *exp.* to be as alike as two peas in a pod • (lit); to be like one egg to the other.

wie ein rohes Ei behandeln (jemanden) *exp.* to handle someone with kid gloves • (lit); to treat someone like a raw egg.

Ende kommt noch (das dicke) *exp.* the worst is yet to come • (lit); the thick end is still coming.

usage example: Der Autounfall war noch nicht das schlimmste. **Das dicke Ende kommt** noch, wenn Karl vor Gericht muß.

translation: The car accident wasn't the worst part. It's going to get worse when Karl has to appear in court.

literal translation: The car accident wasn't the worst part. The thick end is still coming when Karl has to appear in court.

Ende vom Lied (das) *exp.* the outcome, the upshot • (lit); the end of the song.

usage example: **Das Ende vom Lied** war, daß ich nach der Party alles allein aufräumen mußte.

translation: The outcome was that after the party I had to clean up everything by myself.

literal translation: The end of the song was that after the party I had to clean up everything by myself.

Ende gehen (zu) *exp.* to run out (of something) • (lit); to go to the end.

Ende gut, alles gut *exp.* all's well that ends well • (lit); end good, all good.

Ende sein (am) *exp.* to be at the end of one's patience (or power/abilities) • (lit); to be at the end.

falschen Ende anfassen (etwas am) *exp.* to go about something all wrong • (lit); to grasp something at the wrong end.

seinem Leben ein Ende machen/setzen (einer Sacher) *exp.* to put an end to something • (lit); to put/set an end to one's life/something.

es geht um die Wurst *exp.*
do or die, now or never • (lit); it's about the sausage.

usage example: Alle drei Tennisspieler halten den selben Punktestand. Das nächste Spiel bestimmt den Gewinner. Jetzt **geht's um die Wurst**!

translation: Both tennis players are tied. The next game will determine the winner of the match. It's do or die!

literal translation: Both tennis players are tied. The next game will determine the winner of the match. It's for the sausage!

OTHER IDIOMS USING "WURST":

Es ist mir (ganz) Wurst *exp.* I don't give a hoot. • (lit); It's a (total) sausage to me.

etwas ist zu schön, um wahr zu sein *exp.* to be too
good to be true • (lit); [same].

usage example: Ich wünschte, wir könnten ein einziges Mad fliegen, ohne Ärger mit dem Gepäck zu haben. Das wäre doch **zu schön, um wahr zu sein**.

translation: Just once, I wish we could take a plane trip and not have any trouble with the luggage. That would be too good to be true.

literal translation: [same].

Fahrt kommen (in) *exp.* to get into full swing • (lit); come into full drive.

usage example: Frag Opa bloß nicht nach Angelerlebnissen. Wenn er erst einmal **in Fahrt kommt**, hört er nicht wieder auf zu erzählen.

translation: Don't ask grandpa to tell you his fishing stories. Once he starts, he won't stop for a long time.

literal translation: Don't ask grandpa to tell you his fishing stories. Once he gets into full drive, he won't stop for a long time.

Fahrt bringen (jemanden in) *exp.*to get some- one all worked up • (lit); to bring someone in drive.

Fahrt ins Blaue machen (eine) *exp.*to go for a drive • (lit); to make a drive into the blue.

freie Fahrt haben *exp.*to have been given the green light (to do something) • (lit); to have a free way.

voller Fahrt (in) *exp.*at full speed • (lit); in full drive.

Farbe bekennen müssen
exp. to tell the truth, to "fess up", to lay one's cards on the table • (lit); to confess color.

usage example: Gerd mußte **Farbe bekennen**, daß er nicht über Computer bescheid weiß. Er hat gelogen, um den Job zu kriegen.

translation: Gerd had to lay his cards on the table that he really doesn't know anything about computers. He lied about it to get this job.

literal translation: Gerd had to confess color that he really doesn't know anything about computers. He lied about it to get this job.

Fassung bringen (jemanden aus der) *exp.*
to throw someone for a loop • (lit); to bring someone out of one's mounting or frame (in essence, composure).

usage example: Du hast mich völlig **aus der Fassung gebracht** mit deinen Bemerkungen über meine Figur!

translation: You really threw me for a loop with your remarks about my figure!

literal translation: You completely brought me out of composure with your remarks about my figure!

Fassung bewahren/ verlieren *exp.* to keep one's head • (lit); to keep/lose one's composure.

Federlesens machen (nicht viel) *exp.* not to miss a beat (in doing something), without hesitation • (lit); not to pick off many feathers.

usage example: Die Firma machte **nicht viel Federlesens** und feuerte Georg sofort, als er beim Stehlen erwischt wurde.

translation: The company didn't miss a beat and fired George right away when he was caught stealing.

literal translation: The company didn't pick off many feathers and fired George right away when he was caught stealing.

Fettnäpfchen treten (ins)

exp. to put one's foot in one's mouth • (lit); to step in the fat bowl.

usage example: Mit dieser Bemerkung bin ich ganz schön **ins Fettnäpfchen getreten**.

translation: I really put my foot in my mouth with that remark.

literal translation: I really stepped in the fat bowl with that remark.

Fingern abzählen können (sich etwas an allen fünf)

exp. to be able to predict something • (lit); to be able to count something on all five fingers.

usage example: Das hätte ich mir doch **an allen fünf Fingern abzählen** können, daß meine Mutter dieses Hotel nicht mögen würde.

translation: I could have predicted that my mother wasn't going to like this hotel.

literal translation: I could have counted off on all five fingers that my mother wasn't going to like this hotel.

Fingern saugen (sich etwas aus den)

exp. to make something up • (lit); to suck something out of one's fingers.

usage example: Ela sagt, sie hätte Michael Jackson im Supermarket gesehen. Das hat sie sich sicher **aus den Fingern gesogen**.

translation: Ela said that she saw Michael Jackson at the supermarket. I'm sure she made that up.

literal translation: Ela said that she saw Michael Jackson at the supermarket. I'm sure she sucked that out of her fingers.

OTHER IDIOMS USING "FINGER":

Finger geschnitten haben (sich in den)

exp. to have another think coming • (lit); to have cut oneself in the finger.

Finger sehen/gucken (jemandem auf die)

exp. to keep a sharp eye on someone • (lit); to see/look onto someone's fingers.

keinen Finger rühren

exp. not to lift a finger • (lit); not to stir a finger.

kleinen Finger machen (etwas mit dem) *exp.* to do something with one's eyes shut • (lit); to do something with the little finger.

kleinen Finger wickeln (jemanden um den) *exp.* to wrap someone around one's little finger • (lit); to wrap someone around the little finger.

wenn man ihm den kleinen Finger reicht, nimmt er gleich die ganze Hand *exp.* give him an inch, he'll take a mile • (lit); if one extends the little finger to him, he'll take the whole hand.

Flinte nicht ins Korn werfen (die) *exp.* not to throw in the towel • (lit); not to throw the rifle into the corn (field).

usage example: Du darfst einfach **nicht die Flinte ins Korn werfen**. Irgendwann wirst du die Führerscheinprüfung schon bestehen.

translation: You can't just throw in the towel. You'll pass the driver's test eventually.

literal translation: You can't just throw the rifle into the corn (field). You'll pass the driver's test eventually.

Geistern verlassen sein (von allen guten) *exp.* to be out of one's mind • (lit); to be left by all good spirits.

usage example: Bist du **von allen guten Geistern verlassen**? Wenn der Chef dich beim Trinken bei der Arbeit erwischt, schmeißt er dich raus!

translation: Are you out of your mind? If the boss sees you drinking on the job, he'll fire you!

literal translation: Have you been left by all good spirits? If the boss sees you drinking on the job, he'll fire you!

Geld wie Heu haben *exp.* to be filthy rich • (lit); to have money like hay.

usage example: Lothar **hat Geld wie Heu**. Er kauft sich jedes Jahr ein neues Auto!

translation: Lothar is filthy rich. He buys a new car every year!

literal translation: Lothar's got money like hay. He buys a new car every year!

Geld zum Fenster herauswerfen (das) *exp.*

to waste one's money • (lit); to throw one's money out the window.

usage example: Diese Lederjacke ist viel zu teuer, so kann ich mein **Geld auch nicht zum Fenster hinauswerfen**.

translation: That leather jacket is much too expensive. I can't throw my money away like that.

literal translation: That leather jacket is much too expensive. I can't throw my money out of the window like that.

OTHER IDIOMS USING "GELD":

das ist hinausgeworfenes Geld *exp.* that's money down the drain • (lit); that's thrown out money.

Geld machen (etwas zu) *exp.* to turn something into cash • (lit); to make something to money.

Geld scheffeln *exp.* to rake in the money • (lit); to shovel money.

Gelde schwimmen (im) *exp.* to be rolling in money • (lit); to be swimming in money.

große Geld machen (das) *exp.* to make a lot of money • (lit); to make the big money.

Gift nehmen können (auf etwas) *exp.*

to bet one's bottom dollar on something • (lit); to take poison on something.

usage example: "Willst du wirlich deinen Job kündigen?"
"Darauf **kannst du Gift nehmen**! Ich kann meinen Chef nicht mehr ausstehen!"

translation: "Do you really want to quit your job?"
"You better believe it! I can't tolerate my boss any longer!"

literal translation: "Do you really want to quit your job?"
"You can take poison on that! I can't tolerate my boss any longer!"

Glocke hängen (etwas an die große) *exp.*

to spread the news, to broadcast something • (lit); to hang something on a big bell.

usage example: Du solltest doch nicht **an die große Glocke hängen**, daß ich schwanger bin. Ich habe es noch nicht einmal meinen Eltern erzählt!

translation: You weren't supposed to broadcast to everyone that I'm pregnant. I haven't even told my parents yet!

literal translation: You weren't supposed to hang it on a big bell that I'm pregnant. I haven't even told my parents yet!

grün und blau ärgern (sich) *exp.* to be furious, to see red • (lit); to anger oneself green and blue.

usage example: Ich **ärgere mich grün und blau**, daß ich diese Woche kein Lotto gespielt habe. Alle meine Zahlen wurden gezogen!

translation: I'm so furious that I didn't play the lottery this week. All my numbers were drawn!

literal translation: I anger myself green and blue that I didn't play the lottery this week. All my numbers were drawn!

OTHER IDIOMS USING "GRÜN":

grün und blau schlagen (jemanden) *exp.* to beat someone black and blue • (lit); to beat someone green and blue.

Grüne fahren (ins) *exp.* to drive to the country • (lit); to drive into the green.

Grüner (ein) *n.* • **1.** an ecologist, environmentalist • **2.** mucus in one's throat, "loogie" (lit); a green.

Grünes Licht (für etwas) geben/haben *exp.* to give/have the green light to do something • (lit); to give/have a green light (for something).

nicht grün sein (jemandem) *exp.* to have it in for someone • (lit); not to be green to someone.

noch grün hinter den Ohren sein *exp.* inexperienced, wet behind the ears • (lit); to be still green behind the ears.

OTHER IDIOMS USING "BLAU":

blau machen *exp.* to take a day off • (lit); to make blue.

blau sein *exp.* to be drunk, plastered • (lit); to be blue.

blauen Auge davonkommen (mit einem) *exp.* to get off unscathed • (lit); to get away with a blue eye.

blaues Auge (ein) *exp.* a black eye • (lit); a blue eye.

halbem Wege entgegen kommen (jemandem auf) *exp.* to compromise • (lit); to meet someone halfway.

usage example: Ich **komme dir auf halbem Wege entgegen**. Wenn du das Auto zu meinem Preis kaufst, gebe ich dir noch die Stereoanlage dazu.

translation: Let's compromise. If you buy the car at my asking price, I'll throw in the stereo.

literal translation: I'll meet you halfway. If you buy the car at my asking price, I'll throw in the stereo.

OTHER IDIOMS USING "WEG":

besten Weg sein, etwas zu tun (auf dem) *exp.* to be well on the way toward doing something • (lit); to be on the best way to do something.

neue Wege beschreiten/ gehen *exp.* to break new ground • (lit); to tread/walk a new way.

schnellstem Weg(e) (auf) *exp.* as quickly as possible • (lit); on the fastest way.

Weg(e) gehen (jemandem aus dem) *exp.* to keep out of someone's way • (lit); to go out of someone's way.

Weg abkürzen (den) *exp.* to take a short cut • (lit); to shorten the way.

Weg abnehmen (jemandem einen) *exp.* to run an errand for someone • (lit); to take a way off someone.

Weg abschneiden (jemandem den) *exp.* to head someone off • (lit); to cut off someone's way.

Weg des geringsten Widerstands gehen (den) *exp.* to take the path of least resistance • (lit); to go the way of the least resistance.

Weg trauen (jemandem nicht über den) *exp.* not to trust someone at all • (lit); not to trust someone across the way.

Weg der Besserung sein (auf dem) *exp.* to be on the road to recovery • (lit); to be on the way of recovery.

Weg räumen (jemanden/ etwas aus dem) *exp.* to get rid of someone/ something • (lit); to clear something/someone out of the way.

Wege leiten (etwas in die) *exp.* to get something under way • (lit); to direct something on its way.

Hals kriegen (etwas in den falschen) *exp.* to take something the wrong way • (lit); to get something down the wrong throat.

usage example: Was ich über seine Frau gesagt habe, hat er

völlig **in den falschen Hals gekriegt**.

translation: What I said about his wife, he completely took the wrong way.

literal translation: What I said about his wife, he really got down the wrong throat.

OTHER IDIOMS USING "HALS":

aus vollem Halse lachen
exp. to roar with laughter •
(lit); to laugh out of a full throat.

aus vollem Halse schreien *exp.* to shout at the top of one's lungs •
(lit); to yell out of a full throat.

Frosch im Hals haben (einen) *exp.* to have a frog in one's throat • (lit); to have a frog in the throat.

Hals brechen (sich den)
exp. to break one's neck •
(lit); to break one's neck.

Hals umdrehen (jemandem den) *exp.* to wring someone's neck •
(lit); to turn someone's neck around.

Kloß im Hals haben (einen) *exp.* to be speechless • (lit); to have a dumpling in the throat.

Hals und Beinbruch wünschen (jemandem)

exp. to wish someone good luck ("Break a leg!") • (lit); to wish someone a neck and leg fracture ("Neck and leg fracture!").

usage example: Ich höre du hast morgen ein Vorstellungsgespräch. Ich wünsche dir **Hals und Beinbruch**!

translation: I hear you have a job interview tomorrow. Break a leg!

literal translation: I hear you have a job interview tomorrow. Neck and leg fracture!

Haut stecken wollen (nicht in jemandes) *exp.*

not to want to be in someone's shoes • (lit); not to want to be stuck in someone's skin.

usage example: Ich möchte wirklich **nicht in deiner Haut stecken**, wenn Mutti herausfindet, daß du ihr Auto geschrottet hast.

translation: I really wouldn't want to be in your shoes when Mom finds out you wrecked her car.

literal translation: I really wouldn't want to be stuck in your skin when mom finds out that you wrecked her car.

auf der faulen Haut liegen / sich auf die faule Haut legen *exp.* not to lift a finger • (lit); to lie on the lazy skin / to lie down on one's lazy skin.

dicke Haut haben (eine) *exp.* to be thick-skinned • (lit); to have a thick skin.

ehrliche Haut (eine) *exp.* an honest person • (lit); an honest skin.

Haut durchnäßt (bis auf die) *exp.* soaked to the skin • (lit); wet down to the skin.

Haut fahren (aus der) *exp.* to jump out of one's skin • (lit); to drive out of one's skin.

Haut gehen (jemandem unter die) *exp.* to get under someone's skin • (lit); [same].

Haut retten (seine eigene) *exp.* to save one's own skin • (lit); [same].

Haut und Haar (mit) *exp.* completely, entirely • (lit); with skin and hair.

Haut und Knochen sein (nur) *exp.* to be nothing but skin and bones • (lit); to be only skin and bones.

heißen Brei reden (um den) *exp.* to beat around the bush • (lit); to talk around the hot porridge.

usage example: Sag mir einfach was du willst! Hör auf, **um den heißen Brei zu reden**!

translation: Just tell me what you want! Stop beating around the bush!

literal translation: Just tell me what you want! Stop talking around the hot porridge!

zu Brei schlagen (jemanden) *exp.* to beat someone to a pulp • (lit); [same].

herumreiten (auf etwas) *exp.* to go on and on about the same subject • (lit); to ride about on something.

usage example: Es ist wirklich schwer, sich mit Angela zu unterhalten. Sie **reitet** immer nur auf demselben Thema **herum**!

translation: It's so hard talking to Angela. She always goes on and on about the same old thing!

literal translation: It's so hard talking to Angela. She always rides about on the same theme!

"Hat Dich der Teufel geritten?" *exp.* "Have you lost your mind?" • (lit); "Has the devil ridden you?"

Herz total in die Hose gerutscht (jemandem ist das) *exp.* to have one's heart in one's throat • (lit); someone's heart has totally slid in his plants.

usage example: Als ich letzte Nacht Schritte im Haus gehört habe, ist mir **das Herz total in die Hose gerutscht**.

translation: When I heard footsteps in my house last night, my heart suddenly went into my throat.

literal translation: When I heard footsteps in my house last night, my heart suddenly slipped in my pants.

Herz und eine Seele sein (ein) *exp.* to be inseparable • (lit); to be one heart and one soul.

usage example: Es überrascht mich nicht, daß Kurt und Hanna heiraten. Sie waren schon immer **ein Herz und eine Seele** in der Schule.

translation: I'm not surprised that Kurt and Hanna are getting married. They were inseparable back in school.

literal translation: I'm not surprised that Kurt and Hanna are getting married. They were one heart and one soul back in school.

Hand aufs Herz! *exp.* Cross my heart! • (lit); hand on the heart.

Herzensbrecher *exp.* heart breaker • (lit); [same].

herzlos *exp.* heartless • (lit); heartless.

Herzschmerz *exp.* heartache • (lit); heart pain.

Herz auf der Zunge tragen *exp.* to wear one's heart on one's sleeve • (lit); to carry one's heart on the tongue.

Herzen gern (von) *exp.* from the bottom of my heart • (lit); with heart pleasure.

Herzen haben (etwas auf dem) *exp.* to have something on one's mind • (lit); to have something on one's heart.

Kind unter dem Herzen tragen (ein) *exp.* to be with child • (lit); to carry a child below the heart.

Mitten ins Herz *exp.* to be in love • (lit); right in the middle of the heart.

schweren Herzens *exp.* with a heavy heart • (lit); [same].

Stein fiel mir vom Herzen (ein) *exp.* to take a load off one's mind • (lit); a stone fell off my heart.

von ganzem Herzen *exp.* from the bottom of one's heart • (lit); from all of the heart.

Holzweg sein (auf dem)

exp. to be very mistaken • (lit); to be on the wood way.

usage example: Wenn du denkst, daß ich dir noch einmal Geld leihen werde, bist du aber **auf dem Holzweg**.

translation: If you think I'd ever loan you money again, you're very mistaken.

literal translation: If you think I'd ever loan you money again, you're on the wood way.

Hose gehen (in die) *exp.* not

to turn out well • (lit); to go into the pants.

usage example: Meine Zeichnung für den Kunstunterricht ist völlig **in die Hose gegangen**. Es sollte ein Mädchen sein, aber es sieht aus wie eine Birne.

translation: My drawing for art class didn't turn out well. It was supposed to be a girl but it looks like a pear!

literal translation: My drawing for art class went into the pants. It was supposed to be a girl but it looks like a pear!

OTHER IDIOMS USING "HOSE":

Hosen anhaben (die) *exp.* to have the upper hand • (lit); to have the pants on.

Hosenboden setzen (sich auf den) *exp.* to get down to work • (lit); to sit down on one's pants.

Hosen strammziehen (jemandem die) *exp.* to give someone a spanking • (lit); to straighten someone's pants.

Hosen voll haben (die) *exp.* to be scared • (lit); to have the pants full.

Hühnchen mit jemandem zu rupfen haben (ein)

exp. to have a bone to pick with someone • (lit); to have a chicken to pluck with someone.

usage example: Mit dir habe ich noch **ein Hühnchen zu rupfen**, Lise. Wie kommt der Brandfleck in das neue Kleid, das ich dir geborgt hatte?!

translation: I still have a bone to pick with you, Lise. How did the burned spot get on that new dress I lent you?!

literal translation: I still have a chicken to pluck with you, Lise. How did the burned spot get in that new dress I lent you?!

Hund begraben (da liegt der) *exp.* to be the root of one's problem • (lit); that's where the dog lies buried.

usage example: Du nimmst immer Schmalz statt Butter?! Na, **da liegt doch der Hund begraben**. Deshalb werden deine Kuchen nichts.

translation: You're using lard instead of butter?! Well, there's your problem. That's why your cakes don't turn out.

literal translation: You're using lard instead of butter?! Well, there the dog lies buried. That's why your cakes don't turn out.

OTHER IDIOMS USING "HUND":

getroffene Hunde bellen *exp.* said of a guilty person who overacts his innocence • (lit); hit dogs bark.

Hundeleben (ein) *exp.* a dog's life • (lit); [same].

Hunde, die viel bellen, beißen nicht *exp.* Barking dogs seldom bite • (lit); dogs that bark a lot, don't bite.

Hundeelend sein *exp.* to be sick as a dog • (lit); [same].

Karte setzen (alles auf eine) *exp.* to put all one's eggs into one basket • (lit); to bet it all on one card.

usage example: Setze nicht **alles auf eine Karte**! Du solltest dich noch um andere Jobs bemühen, für den Fall, daß du diesen nicht kriegen solltest.

translation: Don't put all your eggs into one basket! You really should apply for some other jobs in case you don't get this one.

literal translation: Don't bet it all on one card! You really should apply for some other jobs in case you don't get this one.

OTHER IDIOMS USING "KARTE":

Karten aufdecken (seine) *exp.* to show one's hand • (lit); to expose one's cards.

gute Karten haben *exp.* to have a good chance • (lit); to have good cards.

Karten sehen (jemandem) (in die) *exp.* to see through someone's game • (lit); to look in someone's cards.

offenen Karten spielen (mit) *exp.* to put one's cards on the table • (lit); to play with open cards.

Keine grauen Haare wachsen lassen (sich)

exp. not to lose sleep over something • (lit); not to grow grey hair over something.

usage example: Man sagt, daß wir eines Tages ein großes Erdbeben haben werden, aber darüber lasse ich mir **keine grauen Haare wachsen**. Wenn es passiert, passiert es eben.

translation: They say that we're going to have a large earthquake some day, but I'm not going to lose any sleep over it. If it happens, it happens.

literal translation: They say that we're going to have a large earthquake some day, but I'm not going to grow any grey hair over it. If it happens, it happens.

OTHER IDIOMS USING "HAAR":

Haar gleichen (jemandem aufs) *exp.* to be the spitting image of someone • (lit); to be like someone to the hair.

Haar in der Suppe finden (ein) *exp.* to knitpick, to find fault with something/someone, to find a fly in the ointment • (lit); to find a hair in the soup.

Haare auf den Zähnen haben *exp.* to be a tough customer • (lit); to have hairs on the teeth.

Haare ausraufen (sich die) *exp.* to tear one's hair out • (lit); [same].

Haare lassen müssen *exp.* **1.** to suffer heavy losses • **2.** to get ripped off • (lit); to have to leave hairs.

Haaren herbeigezogen (an den) *exp.* to be far-fetched • (lit); to be dragged by the hairs.

Haaren liegen (sich in den) *exp.* to be in disagreement • (lit); to lie in one's hairs.

haargenau *adj.* exactly, to a T • (lit); hair exact.

kein gutes Haar an jemandem lassen *exp.* to rip a person to pieces (through criticism) • (lit); not to let a good hair on someone.

Kind beim Namen nennen (das) *exp.* to call a spade a spade • (lit); to call the child by its name.

usage example: O.K. wenn ich **das Kind beim Namen nennen** soll, deine Schwester geht mit einem Schwachkopf aus!

translation: O.K. If I have to call a spade a spade, your sister is going out with a moron!

literal translation: O.K. If I have to call the child by its name, your sister is going out with a weak-head!

NOTE: **Schwachkopf** n. imbecile, moron • (lit); weak-head.

OTHER IDIOMS USING "KIND":

Kind mit dem Badewasser ausschütten (das) *exp.* to throw the baby out with the bath-water • (lit); to pour the baby out with the bath.

unschuldig wie ein neugeborenes Kind sein *exp.* to be as innocent as a new-born baby • (lit); to be as innocent as a new-born child.

klasse sein *exp.* to be first rate, great • (lit); to be (first) class.

usage example: Wir hatten so viel Spaß bei der Wanderung. Es war einfach **klasse**!

translation: We had so much fun hiking. It was just great!

literal translation: We had so much fun hiking. It was just (first) class!

Kopf steht (nicht wissen, wo einem der) *exp.* not to know whether one is coming or going • (lit); not to know where one's head is.

usage example: Ich habe soviel Wäsche zu waschen, ich **weiß gar nicht, wo mir der Kopf steht**!

translation: I've got so much laundry to do, I don't know whether I'm coming or going!

literal translation: I've got so much laundry to do, I don't even know where my head is!

Kopf und Kragen riskieren *exp.* to risk life and limb • (lit); to risk head and neck.

usage example: Hans ist ein Polizist. Er **riskiert täglich Kopf und Kragen**.

translation: Hans is a police officer. He risks life and limb everyday.

literal translation: Hans is a police officer. He risks his head and neck everyday.

Kopfzerbrechen bereiten (sich) *exp.* to worry oneself • (lit); to cause oneself head breakage.

usage example: Manus Spielsucht bereitet mir langsam **Kopfzer- brechen**.

translation: Manu's gambling habit is starting to worry me.

literal translation: Manu's gambling habit is starting to cause me head breakage.

Korb geben (jemandem einen) *exp.* to turn someone down • (lit); to give someone a basket.

usage example: Lotte hat Uwe schon wieder **einen Korb gegeben**. Heute ist einfach nicht sein Tag.

translation: Lotte turned Uwe down again. This is just not his night.

literal translation: Lotte gave Uwe a basket again. This is just not his night.

Lappen gehen (durch die) *exp.* to slip through someone's fingers, to give someone the slip

• (lit); to get through the rags of someone.

usage example: Die Schmugglerbande ist der Grenzpolizei **durch die Lappen gegangen**.

translation: The gang of smugglers managed to slip through the fingers of the border police.

literal translation: The gang of smugglers got through the rags of the border police.

Latein am Ende sein (mit seinem) *exp.* to be at one's wits' end • (lit); to be at the end with one's Latin.

usage example: Dreimal habe ich versucht, Hilde ins Gewissen zu reden, aber sie besteht darauf, eine Tätowierung machen zu lassen. Nun **bin ich mit meinem Latein am Ende**!

translation: I tried three times to talk some sense into Hilde. She still insists on getting a tatoo. I'm at my wits' end!

literal translation: I tried three times to talk some sense into Hilde. She still insists on getting a tatoo. Now I'm at the end with my Latin!

Laus über die Leber gelaufen (jemandem ist eine) *exp.* said of someone who is being bugged by something • (lit); someone had a louse run over his liver.

usage example: Lena hat den ganzen Tag noch nicht einmal gelächelt. Was ihr wohl für **eine Laus über die Leber gelaufen ist**?

translation: Lena didn't smile once all day. What's bugging her?

literal translation: Lena didn't smile once all day. What kind of louse ran across her liver?

OTHER IDIOMS USING "LAUS":

Laus in den Pelz setzen (jemandem eine) *exp.* to give someone problems • (lit); to put a louse in someone's fur.

OTHER IDIOMS USING "LEBER":

frei von der Leber weg reden *exp.* to speak one's mind • (lit); to talk freely from the liver.

Leberwurst spielen (die beleidigte) *exp.* to get in a huff • (lit); to play the pouting liverwurst.

usage example: Greta spielt **die beleidigte Leberwurst**, weil ich ihren Geburtstag vergessen habe.

translation: Greta got in a huff because I forgot her birthday.

literal translation: Greta is playing the offended liverwurst because I forgot her birthday.

Leichen gehen (über) *exp.* to be unscrupulous • (lit); to walk over corpses (to reach one's goal).

usage example: Er hat wirklich kein Gewissen. Er würde **über Leichen gehen**, nur um sein Ziel zu erreichen.

translation: He's got no conscience whatsoever. He would do absolutely anything to reach his goal.

literal translation: He's got no conscience whatsoever. He would walk over corpses to reach his goal.

Leviten lesen (jemandem die) *exp.* to read someone the riot act • (lit); to read to someone from the book of Leviticus (biblical).

usage example: Der Hund hat schon wieder auf den Teppich gepinkelt? Ihm **lese ich jetzt aber kräftig die Leviten**!

translation: The dog peed on the carpet again? I'm gonna read him the riot act now!

literal translation: The dog peed on the carpet again? I'm gonna read him the book of Leviticus now!

Lied davon singen können (ein) *exp.* to know a lot about • (lit); to be able to sing a song about something.

usage example: Eine Grundschulklasse zu unterrichten ist nicht einfach. **Davon kann** ich, als Lehrerin, ein **Lied singen**.

translation: Teaching a class of first graders isn't easy. As a teacher, I know all about it

literal translation: Teaching a class of first graders isn't easy. As a teacher, I can sing a song about it.

links liegen lassen (etwas) *exp.* to pass something up • (lit); to leave something to the left.

usage example: Schwalli kann einfach nichts Süßes **links liegen lassen**, deshalb ist er so dick.

translation: Schwalli can't pass up sweets. That's why he's so big.

literal translation: Schwalli can't leave sweets lying to the left. That's why he's so big.

ALSO: **links liegen lassen (jemanden)** *exp.* to give someone the cold shoulder.

losmachen (einen) *exp.* to paint the town red • (lit); to make one loose.

usage example: Heute Abend gehen wir alle zusammen aus. Da werden wir so richtig **einen losmachen**!

translation: Tonight we're all going out together. We're really going to paint the town red!

literal translation: Tonight we're all going out together. We're really going to untie one!

Marsch blasen (jemandem den) *exp.* to reprimand someone • (lit); to blow someone the march.

usage example: Jetzt reichts! Schulze hat mir schon wieder die Einfahrt zugeparkt. Dem werde ich **den Marsch blasen**!

translation: That does it! Schulze blocked my driveway again. I'm gonna let him have it!

literal translation: That does it! Schulze blocked my driveway again. I'm gonna blow him the march!

Miststück *exp.* (insulting term used for especially for a woman) dirtbag • (lit); piece of manure.

usage example: Petra, dieses **Miststück**, hat mich beim Rektor verraten!

translation: Petra, that dirtbag, told the principal on me!

literal translation: Petra, that piece of manure, told the principal on me!

Misthaufen *exp.* pigsty • (lit); heap of manure.

Mund gefallen sein (nicht auf den) *exp.* not to be at a loss for words • (lit); not to be fallen on one's mouth.

usage example: Ursula ist nicht gerade **auf den Mund gefallen**. Während der Versammlung wußte sie stets, was sie zu sagen hatte.

translation: Ursula is never at a loss for words. During the meeting, she always knew what to say.

literal translation: Ursula never fell on her mouth. During the meeting, she always knew what to say.

in aller Munde (sein) *exp.* everyone's talking about… • (lit); to be in everyone's mouth.

Mund halten (den) *exp.* to shut up • (lit); to hold the mouth.

Mund über etwas halten (seinen) *exp.* to keep something secret • (lit); to keep one's mouth shut about something.

Mund reden (jemandem nach dem) *exp.* to butter someone up • (lit); to talk after someone's mouth.

Mund verbrennen (sich den) *exp.* to put one's foot in one's mouth • (lit); to burn one's mouth.

Mund verziehen (seinen/den) *exp.* to make a face • (lit); to warp one's/the mouth.

Mund wäßrig machen (jemandem den) *exp.* to make someone's mouth water • (lit); [same].

Munde riechen (aus dem) *exp.* to have bad breath • (lit); to smell from the mouth.

mundfaul sein *adj.* not to be talkative • (lit); to be mouth lazy.

mundgerecht *adj.* bite-size
• (lit); mouth just (or: just
made for the mouth).

**Nagel auf den Kopf
treffen (den)** *exp.* to be
absolutely correct • (lit); to hit
the nail on the head.

usage example: Ich glaube, du
hast **den Nagel auf den
Kopf getroffen** als du sagtest,
der Film sei völlig idiotisch.

translation: I think you had it
exactly right when you said the
film was totally idiotic.

literal translation: I think you hit
the nail on the head when you
said the film was totally idiotic.

OTHER IDIOMS USING "NAGEL":

**Nagel hängen (etwas an
den)** *exp.* to give
something up • (lit); to
hang something on the nail.

nigelnagelneu *exp.*
brand-new • (lit); nail-new.

OTHER IDIOMS USING "KOPF":

Dickkopf *n.* a stubborn
person • (lit); thick head.

Dummkopf *n.* moron • (lit);
dumb head.

**durch den Kopf gehen
lassen (sich etwas)**
exp. to think something
over • (lit); to let something
go through one's head.

**es geht um Kopf und
Kragen** *exp.* it's a matter
of life and death • (lit); it
goes for head and neck.

Kopf an Kopf *exp.* neck
and neck • (lit); head to
head.

**Kopf einrennen (sich
den)** *exp.* to beat one's
head against a wall • (lit);
to run one's head into
something.

**Kopf hinhalten
[müssen] (den)** *exp.* to
have to face the music •
(lit); to have to offer one's
head.

**Kopf oben behalten
(den)** *exp.* to keep up
one's spirits • (lit); to keep
the head up.

**Kopf stellen (etwas auf
den)** *exp.* to turn
something upside-down •
(lit); to put something on
the head.

**Kopf waschen
(jemandem den)** *exp.* to
tell someone off • (lit); to
wash someone's head.

Kopf zu sagen (jemandem etwas auf den) *exp.* to tell someone something directly • (lit); to tell someone something to the head.

Kopflastig *n.* intellectual • (lit); head heavy.

nicht auf den Kopf spucken lassen (sich) *exp.* not to let people walk all over oneself • (lit); not to let oneself be spit upon the head.

schweren Kopf haben *exp.* **1.** to have a hangover • **2.** to have a headache • (lit); to have a heavy head.

Narren aus jemandem machen (einen) *exp.* to make a fool out of someone • (lit); [same].

usage example: Warum bestehst du darauf, daß ich diese gräßliche Schlaghose anziehe? Willst du **einen Narren aus mir machen**?!

translation: Why do you insist on me wearing those ugly bell bottom pants? Do you want me to look ridiculous?!

literal translation: Why do you insist on me wearing those ugly bell bottom pants? Do you want to make a fool out of me?!

OTHER IDIOMS USING "NARR":

Narren gefressen haben an (etwas/ jemandem) (einen) *exp.* to be infatuated with something/ someone • (lit); to have eaten a fool on something/someone.

Narren halten (jemanden zum) *exp.* to pull the wool over someone's eyes • (lit); to have/keep someone for a fool.

Nase in alles stecken (seine) *exp.* to be nosey • (lit); to put one's nose into everything.

usage example: Ich kann meinen neuen Nachbarn nicht leiden. Er muß immer **seine Nase in alles stecken**.

translation: I don't like my new neighbor. He's always so nosey.

literal translation: I don't like my new neighbor. He always puts his nose into everything.

Nase von etwas/jemandem voll haben (die) *exp.* to be fed up, to have had all one can tolerate • (lit); to have the nose full of something or someone.

usage example: Wanda hat ihren Freund zum zweiten Mal beim fremdgehen erwischt. Nun hat sie endgültig **die Nase von ihm voll**!

translation: Wanda caught her boyfriend cheating on her for the second time. Now she's completely had it with him!

literal translation: Wanda caught her boyfriend cheating on her for the second time. Now she's had the nose full of him!

OTHER IDIOMS USING "NASE":

es liegt vor deiner Nase
exp. it's right under your nose • (lit); it lies before your nose.

feine Nase haben (eine)
exp. to have a flair for something • (lit); to have a fine nose.

lange Nase machen (jemandem eine) *exp.*
to thumb one's nose at someone • (lit); to make someone a long nose.

Nase binden (jemandem etwas auf die) *exp.* to get something off one's chest • (lit); to tie something on someone's nose.

Nase hochtragen (die)
exp. to have one's nose in the air, to be conceited • (lit); to carry the nose high.

Nase in alles stecken (seine) *exp.* to poke one's nose into someone else's business • (lit); to put one's nose into everything.

Nase liegen (auf der)
exp. to be laid up (sick) • (lit); to lie on the nose.

Nase reiben (jemandem etwas unter die) *exp.*
to rub someone's nose in something • (lit); to rub something under someone's nose.

Nase vorn haben (die)
exp. to be a step ahead, to be in the know • (lit); to have the nose in front.

Naseweis *n.* a nosey person • (lit); nose-know.

Tür vor der Nase zuwerfen (jemandem die) *exp.* to slam the door in someone's face • (lit); to slam the door in front of the nose.

Nerven gehen (jemandem auf die) *exp.* to annoy someone • (lit); to go on one's nerves.

usage example: Das ist schon das fünfte Mal, daß du dasselbe Lied spielst. Es geht mir **auf die Nerven**!

translation: That's the fifth time you've played the same song. It's bothering me!

literal translation: That's the fifth time you've played the same song. It goes on my nerves!

letzten Nerv rauben (jemandem den) *exp.* to try one's patience • (lit); to steal someone's last nerve.

Nerven haben *exp.* to have nerve • (lit); to have nerves.

Nerven verlieren (die) *exp.* to lose one's temper or to lose one's nerves • (lit); to lose the nerves.

Nerven wie Drahtseile haben *exp.* to have nerves of steel • (lit); to have nerves like steel cables.

Nummer sicher gehen (auf) *exp.* to be on the safe side • (lit); to get to number safe.

usage example: Bevor du deinen Aufsatz abgibst, lies ihn dir lieber nochmal durch, um **auf Nummer sicher zu gehen**.

translation: Before you hand in your essay to the teacher, you'd better proofread it again just to be on the safe side.

literal translation: Before you hand in your essay to the teacher, you'd better proofread it again just to get to number safe.

etwas/jemand is eine Nummer zu groß für dich *exp.* said of someone who bites off more than he can chew • (lit); something/someone is one number too big for you.

Nummer sein (eine) *exp.* to be quite a number, to be a real character • (lit); to be a number.

Ohr hauen (jemanden über das) *exp.* to take advantage of someone • (lit); to hit someone over the ear.

usage example: Der Gebrauchtwagenhändler hat dich wirklich **übers Ohr gehauen**. Kein Auto ist $100.000 wert!

translation: That used car salesman really took advantage of you. No car is worth $100,000!

literal translation: That used car salesman really hit you over the ear. No car is worth $100,000!

Ohren schreiben (sich etwas hinter die) *exp.* to get something into one's (thick) head • (lit); to write something behind one's ears.

usage example: Du mußt dir **hinter die Ohren schreiben**, den Ölstand in deinem Auto zu beachten, sonst ruinierst du noch den Motor.

translation: You've got to get it into your head that you have to pay attention to the oil level in your car. If you don't, you're going to ruin the motor!

literal translation: You've got to write it behind your ears that you have to pay attention to the oil level in your car. If you don't, you're going to ruin the motor!

Ohren steif halten (die)

exp. to keep a stiff upper lip • (lit); to keep the ears stiff.

usage example: Ich bin sicher, daß die Polizei deinen Bruder finden wird. **Halt die Ohren steif** und hoffe auf das Beste.

translation: I'm sure the police will find your brother. Keep a stiff upper lip and hope for the best.

literal translation: I'm sure the police will find your brother. Keep the ears stiff and hope for the best.

OTHER IDIOMS USING "OHR":

"Es ist mir zu Ohren gekommen" *exp.* "It has come to my attention" • (lit); It has come to my ears

"Mir klingen die Ohren" *exp.* "My ears are ringing." • (lit); My ears are sounding.

bis über beide Ohren verliebt sein in jemanden *exp.* to be head over heels in love with someone • (lit); to be in love with someone over both ears.

bis über die Ohren *exp.* to be up to one's ears (in something) • (lit); up over the ears.

Bohnen/Petersilie in den Ohren haben *exp.* to turn a deaf ear to something • (lit); to have beans/parsley in the ears.

ganz Ohr sein *exp.* to be all ears • (lit); to be all ear.

grün hinter den Ohren sein *exp.* to be wet behind the ears • (lit); to be green behind the ears.

offenes Ohr finden (ein) *exp.* to find a sympathetic ear • (lit); to find an open ear.

**Ohr haben für etwas
(ein)** *exp.* to have an ear
for something • (lit); [same].

**Ohr hinein, zum andern
hinaus (zum einen)**
exp. in one ear and out the
other • (lit); [same].

Ohr legen (sich aufs)
exp. to take a nap • (lit); to
lie on one's ear.

**Ohr zum andern
grinsen (von einem)**
exp. to smile from ear to
ear • (lit); to grin from one
ear to the other.

**Ohren hängen lassen
(die)** *exp.* to lose heart •
(lit); to leave the ears
hanging.

**Ohren liegen
(jemandem in den)**
exp. to bug someone
relentlessly about
something • (lit); to lie in
someone's ears.

Ohren spitzen (die) *exp.*
to prick up one's ears •
(lit); to sharpen one's ears.

**tauben Ohren predigen
(vor)** *exp.* to preach to
deaf ears • (lit); [same].

**übers Ohr hauen
(jemanden)** *exp.* to put
one over on someone •
(lit); to hit someone over
the ear.

**Wände haben Ohren
(die)** *exp.* the walls have
ears • (lit); [same].

**Pudel dastehen (wie ein
begossener)** *exp.* to look
depressed, pitiful • (lit); to stand
there like a soaked poodle.

usage example: Ich weiß, du hast
den Wein nicht mit Absicht
verschüttet! Jetzt stehe nicht
**da, wie ein begossener
Pudel**. Wir holen eine andere
Flasche aus dem Keller.

translation: I know you didn't
spill the wine on purpose! Don't
stand there looking so
depressed. We'll get another
bottle from the cellar.

literal translation: I know you
didn't spill the wine on purpose!
Don't stand there like a soaked
poodle. We'll get another bottle
from the cellar.

Rad am Wagen sein (das fünfte) *exp.* to feel like a third wheel • (lit); to feel like the fifth wheel on a cart.

usage example: Warum hast du mir nicht gesagt, daß dein Freund mit uns zum Konzert kommt? Ich fühle mich wie **das fünfte Rad am Wagen**!

translation: Why didn't you tell me your boyfriend was going with us to the concert? I feel completely out of place!

literal translation: Why didn't you tell me your boyfriend was going with us to the concert? I feel just like the fifth wheel on a cart!

OTHER IDIOMS USING "RAD":

Rad abhaben (ein) *exp.* to have a screw loose • (lit); to have wheel off.

Räder kommen (unter die) *exp.* to go to the dogs • (lit); to come under the wheels.

OTHER IDIOMS USING "WAGEN":

Wagen fahren (jemandem an den) *exp.* to tread on someone's toes • (lit); to drive on one's wagon.

reinen Tisch machen *exp.* to clear the air • (lit); to clear the table.

usage example: Dein Schweigen kann ich nicht länger ertragen. Laß uns das Geschehene besprechen und **reinen Tisch machen**.

translation: I can't stand your silence any longer. Let's talk about what happened and clear the air.

literal translation: I can't stand your silence any longer. Let's talk about what happened and clear the table.

OTHER IDIOMS USING "TISCH":

Tisch bitten (jemanden zu) *exp.* to request someone to the table • (lit); [same].

Tisch ziehen (jemanden über den) *exp.* to take someone to the cleaners • (lit); to pull someone over the table.

Tisch fallen lassen (etwas unter den) *exp.* not to bring something up • (lit); to let something drop under the table.

ruhige Kugel schieben (eine) *exp.* to kick back and relax • (lit); to push a calm ball.

usage example: Am Sonntag habe ich nichts zu tun. Ich

glaube, da werde **ich eine ruhige Kugel schieben**.

translation: I've got nothing to do on Sunday. I think I'll just kick back and relax.

literal translation: I've got nothing to do on Sunday. I think I'll just push a calm ball.

Saiten aufziehen (andere)
exp. to come down on someone, to get tough with someone • (lit); to put on a different set of strings.

usage example: Wenn Klaus sich nicht bald daran gewöhnt, sein Zimmer aufzuräumen, werden seine Eltern **andere Saiten aufziehen** müssen.

translation: If Klaus doesn't get into the habit of cleaning his room soon, his parents will have to get tough with him.

literal translation: If Klaus doesn't get into the habit of cleaning his room soon, his parents will have to put on a different set of strings.

Sand setzen (etwas in den)
exp. to fail something miserably • (lit); to set something in the sand.

usage example: Ich glaube, ich habe die Mathearbeit völlig **in den Sand gesetzt**.

translation: I think I completely failed the math test.

literal translation: I think I really set the math test in the sand.

SYNONYM: **ein Griff ins Klo**
exp. • (lit); grip into the toilet bowl.

OTHER IDIOMS USING "SAND":

Sande verlaufen (im)
exp. to fizzle out • (lit); to get lost in the sand.

Schlag ins Wasser (ein)
exp. to be a complete flop • (lit); to be a hit in the water.

usage example: Die Büroparty war ein voller **Schlag ins Wasser**. Nur der Hausmeister kam!

translation: The office party was a compete flop. Only the janitor showed up!

literal translation: The office party was a hit in the water. Only the janitor showed up!

OTHER IDIOMS USING "SCHLAG":

keinen Schlag tun *exp.* not to do an ounce (of work) • (lit); not to do a stroke (of work).

Schlag (auf einen) *exp.* all at once • (lit); in one blow.

Schlag (weg)haben (einen) *exp.* to be crazy • (lit); to be a blow/hit short.

Schlag auf Schlag *exp.* in rapid succession • (lit); blow after blow [or] hit after hit.

Schlag ins Gesicht sein (ein) *exp.* to be a slap in the face • (lit); [same].

Schlag versetzen (jemandem einen) *exp.* to deal someone a real blow • (lit); to give someone a stroke/blow/hit.

Schläge kriegen *exp.* to get a thrashing • (lit); to receive a beating.

vernichtenden Schlag gegen jemanden führen (einen) *exp.* to deal someone a crushing blow • (lit); [same].

Schmuddel *n.* a messy person • (lit); see note below.

usage example: Günter war schon immer ein **Schmuddel**. Jetzt hat er sich endlich entschlossen, sein Talent zu nutzen, und Pennbruder zu werden.

translation: Günter always was a filthy person. Now he finally decided to make use of his talent and become a bum.

NOTE: This comes from the word **schmutz** meaning "dirt."

schnallen (etwas nicht) *exp.* not to understand something, not to catch on • (lit); not to buckle something.

usage example: Unsere Lehrerin hat uns die Matheaufgabe noch einmal erklärt, aber Eva hat sie immer noch **nicht geschnallt**.

translation: Our teacher explained the math problem again, but Eva still didn't get it.

literal translation: Our teacher explained the math problem again, but Eva still has not buckled it.

Schnitzer machen (einen groben) *exp.* to make a big screw up, to blow it • (lit); to allow oneself a rough wood cut.

usage example: Da ist mir aber **ein grober Schnitzer** passiert, als ich versuchte, diese junge Frau auf der Party zu küssen. Es stellte sich heraus, daß es die Frau vom Chef war!

translation: I really blew it when I tried to kiss that young woman at the party. She turned out to be the boss's wife!

literal translation: I allowed myself a rough wood cut when I tried to kiss that young woman

at the party. She turned out to
be the boss's wife!

Schraube locker haben (eine) *exp.* to be crazy • (lit); to have a screw loose.

usage example: Bei Petra ist
doch **eine Schraube locker**.
Sie geht am liebsten an den
Strand wenn es regnet.

translation: Petra's weird. She
prefers going to the beach when
it's raining.

literal translation: Petra's got a
screw loose. She prefers going
to the beach when it's raining.

OTHER IDIOMS USING "SCHRAUBE":

Preise in die Höhe schrauben (die) *exp.*to
push prices up • (lit); to
screw or spiral prices in to
heigher elevations.

Senf dazugeben (seinen) *exp.* to add one's two cents • (lit); to add one's mustard.

usage example: Auf der Party
mußte Barbara zu jeder
Angelegenheit ihren **Senf
dazugeben**.

translation: At the party Barbara
had to add her two cents to
every topic.

literal translation: At the party
Barbara had to add her mustard
to every topic.

Spieß umdrehen (den) *exp.* to turn the tables • (lit); to turn the skewer around.

usage example: Helmut hat mich
beschuldigt, unnötig viel Wasser
beim Duschen zu verbrauchen.
Da hab ich **den Spieß** einfach
umgedreht, und ihn an sein
stundenlanges Autowaschen
erinnert.

translation: Helmut accused me
of wasting water while
showering. So, I turned the
tables and reminded him of his
lengthy car washes.

literal translation: Helmut
accused me of wasting water
while showering. So, I turned the
skewer around and reminded
him of his lengthy car washes.

OTHER IDIOMS USING "SPIEß":

Spießer *exp.* bourgeois,
stuck-up person • (lit); one
who pierces.

Spielverderber sein *exp.* to be a kill-joy • (lit); to be a game-spoiler.

usage example: Mußt du so ein
Spielverderber sein? Warum
hast du die Musik ausgemacht?
Wir hatten soviel Spaß beim
Tanzen.

translation: Do you have to be
such a kill-joy? Why did you turn
the music off? We were having
so much fun dancing.

literal translation: Do you have to be such a game-spoiler? Why did you turn the music off? We were having so much fun dancing.

Spinner *exp.* screwball • (lit); loon.

usage example: Karl ist ein totaler **Spinner**. Er gießt seinen Garten, obwohl es regnet.

translation: Karl's a total nut. He's watering his garden even though it's raining.

literal translation: Karl is a total loon. He's watering his garden even though it's raining.

spitze *exp.* the best • (lit); the peak.

usage example: Das Rolling Stones Konzert war einfach **spitze**!

translation: The Rolling Stones concert was totally awsome!

literal translation: The Rolling Stones concert was the absolute peak!

OTHER IDIOMS USING "SPITZE":

Spitze liegen (an der) *exp.* to be in the lead, first place (sports) • (lit); to lie at the peak.

Spitze treiben etwas (auf die) *exp.* to carry things too far • (lit); to drive to the peak of something.

Stange bleiben (bei der) *exp.* to stick to doing something • (lit); to stay at the pole.

usage example: Du kannst schon einige Lieder auf der Gitarre spielen, und wenn du jetzt **bei der Stange** bleibst, spielst du bald wie ein Profi!

translation: You're starting to play the guitar very well. If you stick to it, some day you'll be able to play like a pro!

literal translation: You're starting to play the guitar very well. If you stay at the pole, some day you'll be able to play like a pro!

OTHER IDIOMS USING "STANGE":

Bohnenstange *exp.* tall person • (lit); bean pole.

schöne Stange Geld (eine) *exp.* a nice sum of money • (lit); a nice pole of money.

Stange (von der) *exp.* off-the-rack • (lit); off the pole.

Stange halten (jemandem) (die) *exp.* to stick up for someone • (lit); to hold someone's pole.

Stein im Brett haben (bei jemandem einen) *exp.* to be in one's good graces • (lit); to have a stone in the board with someone.

usage example: Mein Vater hat bei meiner Oma einen **Stein im Brett**, weil er ihr immer im Garten hilft.

translation: My father is in good graces with my grandma because he always helps her with her garden.

literal translation: My father has a stone in the board with my grandma because he always helps her with her garden.

OTHER IDIOMS USING "STEIN":

ersten Stein werfen (den) *exp.* to cast the first stone • (lit); [same].

man soll nicht mit Steinen werfen, wenn man selbst in Glashaus sitzt *exp.* people who sit in glass houses shouldn't throw stones • (lit); one should not throw stones when one sits by oneself in a glass house.

Stein des Anstoßes *exp.* a stumbling-block • (lit); the stone of initiative.

Stein ins Rollen bringen (den) *exp.* to get the ball rolling • (lit); to get the stone rolling.

Streit vom Zaun brechen (einen) *exp.* to start an argument • (lit); to break an argument off the fence.

usage example: Irene braucht keinen Grund um **einen Streit vom Zaun zu brechen**. Ich glaube, sie zankt sich einfach gern.

translation: Irene doesn't need a reason to start an argument. I think she really loves to fight.

literal translation: Irene doesn't need a reason to break an argument off the fence. I think she really loves to fight.

OTHER IDIOMS USING "STREIT":

Streit liegen (mit jemandem in) *exp.* to be at odds with someone • (lit); to lie in argument with someone.

Streithahn *n.* one who argues a lot • (lit); argument rooster.

Tante *exp.* (derogatory) woman/girl, chick • (lit); aunt.

usage example: Die **Tante** an der Abendkasse hat mir falsches Wechselgeld herausgegeben!

translation: The chick at the box office didn't give me enough change back!

literal translation: The aunt at the box office didn't give me the correct change!

Teufel scheren (zum) *exp.*
to get lost • (lit); to go to the devil.

usage example: Nachdem Schröder mehrere Male betrunken am Arbeitsplatz erschienen ist, sagte ihm der Vorarbeiter ihm, er solle sich **zum Teufel scheren**.

translation: After showing up drunk at work several times, Schröder's supervisor told him to get lost.

literal translation: After showing up drunk at work several times, Schröder's supervisor told him to go to the devil.

Tode langweilen (sich zu)
exp. to bore one greatly • (lit); to bore one to death.

usage example: Ins Museum zu gehen, **langweilt mich zu Tode**.

translation: Going to museums bores me greatly!

literal translation: Going to museums bores me to death!

Tod holen (sich den) *exp.* to catch one's death • (lit); to get one's death.

Tod nicht leiden können (jemanden/etwas auf den) *exp.* to hate someone/something • (lit); not to be able to bare someone up to death.

Tod finden (den) *exp.* to meet one's death • (lit); to find death.

Tode lachen (sich zu) *exp.* to laugh oneself silly • (lit); to laugh oneself to death.

Tode trinken/arbeiten (sich zu) *exp.* to drink/work oneself to death • (lit); [same].

Todesangst *exp.* scared to death • (lit); [same].

Todesstille *exp.* dead silence • (lit); [same].

Ton vergreifen (sich im)
exp. to blow it • (lit); to hit the wrong note.

usage example: Hubert hat sich wirklich **im Ton vergriffen**, als er seinen Boss einen Idioten nannte.

translation: Hubert really blew it when he called his boss an idiot.

literal translation: Hubert really grabbed the wrong note when he called his boss an idiot.

gehört zum guten Ton (etwas) *exp.* to be according to protocol • (lit); something belonging to the good tone.

in höchsten Tönen von jemandem/etwas reden *exp.* to speak highly about someone/something • (lit); to speak in highest tones about someone/ something.

Ton angeben (den) *exp.* to set the tone (in a conversation) • (lit); [same].

totlachen (sich) *exp.* to laugh hard • (lit); to laugh oneself to death.

usage example: Über den Film könnte ich mich **totlachen**!

translation: I can't stop laughing over that movie!

literal translation: I could laugh myself to death over that movie!

da gibt es gar nichts zu lachen *exp.* it's no laughing matter • (lit); there's nothing to laugh about.

die Sonne lacht *exp.* the sun is shining brightly • (lit); the sun is laughing.

platzen/sterben vor Lachen *exp.* to split one's sides laughing • (lit); to burst/die of laughter.

wer zuletzt lacht, lacht am besten *exp.* he who laughs last, laughs longest • (lit); he who laughs last, laughs best.

Traum einfallen lassen (sich etwas nicht im) *exp.* to be inconceivable • (lit); not to think of doing something in one's dreams.

usage example: Es würde mir **im Traum nicht einfallen**, mit Dieter auszugehen. Er ist so komisch!

translation: I'd never consider of going out with Dieter. He's so weird!

literal translation: I'd never dream of going out with Dieter. He's so weird!

verputzen (etwas) *exp.* to devour something • (lit); to polish off something.

usage example: Olaf hat den ganzen Truthahn allein **verputzt**. Wo steckt er das nur hin?

translation: Olaf ate the whole turkey by himself. Where does he put it?

literal translation: Olaf polished off the whole turkey by himself. Where does he put it?

OTHER IDIOMS USING "VERPUTZEN":

verputzen können (jemanden nicht) *exp.* to be unable to stand someone • (lit); not to be able to digest someone.

viel um die Ohren haben

exp. to be very busy, to be up to one's ears in work • (lit); to have much around the ears.

usage example: Das Telefon klingelt pausenlos! Ich **habe zuviel um die Ohren**!

translation: The phone's been ringing endlessly! I'm too busy!

literal translation: The phone's been ringing endlessly! I have too much around the ears!

"Was gibt's?" *exp.* "What's happening?" • (lit); "What gives?"

usage example: **Was gibt's**? Lange nicht gesehen!

translation: What's up? Long time no see!

literal translation: What gives? Long time no see!

OTHER IDIOMS USING "GEBEN":

da gibt's nichts *exp.* there's no doubt about it • (lit); there's nothing.

Fest geben (ein) *exp.* to throw a party • (lit); to give a feast.

ganze Liebe geben (jemandem seine) *exp.* to give someone all one's love • (lit); to give someone all of one's love.

geben (es sich) *exp.* • **1.** to get drunk • **2.** to put someone down • **3.** to beat oneself up (over something) • (lit); to give it to oneself.

geben (etwas von sich) *exp.* to utter something • (lit); to give something of oneself.

Hand geben (etwas [nicht] aus der) *exp.* not to let go of something • (lit); [not] to give something out of the hand.

Hand geben (jemandem die) *exp.* to shake someone's hand • (lit); to give someone the hand.

Hand geben (jemandem etwas in die) *exp.* to give someone something • (lit); to give someone something in the hand.

keinen Laut/Ton von sich geben *exp.* not to make a sound • (lit); not to give a sound/tone.

Reparatur geben (etwas in) *exp.* to take something in to be repaired • (lit); to give something to repair.

übergeben (sich) *exp.* to throw up • (lit); to overgive

was gibt es Neues? *exp.* what's new? • (lit); what gives it new?

wer gibt? *exp.* whose deal is it? (cards) / whose serve is it? (sports) • (lit); who gives?

Wort gab das andere (ein) *exp.* one word led to another • (lit); one word gave the other.

Wassern gewaschen sein (mit allen) *exp.* to know all the tricks of the trade • (lit); to be washed with all the waters.

usage example: Mein Steuerberater **ist mit allen Wassern gewaschen**. Er kann dir bestimmt mit deinem Steuerproblem helfen.

translation: My accountant knows all the tricks of the trade. He can certainly help you with your tax problem.

literal translation: My accountant is washed with all the waters. He can certainly help you with your tax problem.

OTHER IDIOMS USING "WASSER":

Schlag ins Wasser (ein) *exp.* to be a complete flop • (lit); to be a hit in the water.

stille Wasser gründen tief *exp.* still waters run deep • (lit); silent waters are grounded deeply.

Wasser abgraben (jemandem) (das) *exp.* to pull the carpet from under someone's feet • (lit); to dig someone's water off.

Wasser fallen (ins) *exp.* to fall through • (lit); to fall in the water.

Wasser halten (sich über) *exp.* to keep one's head above water • (lit); to keep oneself above water.

Wasser reichen können (jemandem nicht das) *exp.* not to be able to hold a candle to someone • (lit); not to be able to pass the water to someone.

Wässerchen trüben können (kein) *exp.* to look very innocent, to look like butter wouldn't melt in one's mouth • (lit); not to be able to cloud waters.

usage example: Fritz sieht aus, als ob er **kein Wässerchen trüben könnte**. Dabei haben seine Lehrer aber viel mit ihm zu schaffen.

translation: Fritz looks so innocent but his teachers have a lot of trouble with him.

literal translation: Fritz looks like he could cloud no waters, but his teachers have a lot of trouble with him.

Wein einschenken (jemandem reinen) *exp.* to give it to someone straight • (lit); to pour someone pure wine.

usage example: Jemand muß Franz endlich **reinen Wein einschenken**, und ihm sagen, daß er gekündigt ist.

translation: Someone's finally got to give it to Franz straight and tell him he's fired.

literal translation: Someone has to pour Franz pure wine and tell him he's fired.

weismachen wollen (jemandem/etwas) *exp.* to pull the wool over someone's eyes • (lit); to want to make someone/something wise.

usage example: Marie **wollte mir weismachen**, daß ihre Familie königlicher Abstammung ist.

translation: Marie tried to pull the wool over my eyes by telling me that her family is actually royalty.

literal translation: Marie wanted to make me wise that her family is actually of royal descent.

Westentasche kennen (etwas wie seine) *exp.* to be very familiar with something (especially a location), to know something like the back of one's hand • (lit); to know something like one's vest pocket.

usage example: Was macht Hugo so in seiner Freizeit? Laß uns einfach mal sagen er kennt den Rotlichtbezirk **wie seine Westentasche**.

translation: What does Hugo do in his spare time? Let's just say he knows his way around the red light district.

literal translation: What does Hugo do in his spare time? Let's just say he knows the red light district like his vest pocket.

Wink mit dem Zaunpfahl (ein) *exp.* a broad hint • (lit); a hint with the fencepost.

usage example: Ich glaube das sollte **ein Wink mit dem Zaunpfahl** sein, als Elli sagte, sie sei in das Kleid im Schaufenster verliebt.

translation: I think Elli was dropping a broad hint when she said she was in love with the dress in the window.

literal translation: I think it was supposed to be a hint with the fencepost when Elli said she was in love with the dress in the window.

Wort auf die Goldwaage legen (nicht jedes) *exp.* to hang on one's every word • (lit); to put every word on the gold (jeweler's) scale.

usage example: In einem Scheidungsfall wird **jedes Wort auf die Goldwaage gelegt**.

translation: In a divorce case, they'll hang on every word.

literal translation: In a divorce case, every single word will be put on the gold (jeweler's) scale.

OTHER IDIOMS USING "WORT":

anderen Worten (mit) *exp.* in other words • (lit); with other words.

beim Wort nehmen *exp.* to take someone up on one's offer • (lit); to take at the word.

gutes Wort einlegen (für jemanden ein) *exp.* to put in a good word for someone • (lit); [same].

keinem Wort erwähnen (etwas mit) *exp.* not to say a word about something • (lit); to mention something without words.

nicht zu Wort kommen *exp.* not to get a word in edgewise • (lit); not to get to the word.

ohne viele Worte zu machen *exp.* without further ado • (lit); without making many words.

paar Worte sprechen (ein) *exp.* to make a toast • (lit); to speak a few words.

sein Wort brechen *exp.* to break one's word • (lit); [same].

"Spar dir deine Worte!" *exp.* "Don't waste your breath!" • (lit); Save your words!

Wort aus dem Munde nehmen (jemandem das) *exp.* to take the words out of someone's mouth • (lit); [same].

Wort fallen (jemandem ins) *exp.* to cut someone short • (lit); to fall into someone's word.

Wort haben (das) *exp.* to have the floor • (lit); to have the word.

Wort halten *exp.* to keep one's word • (lit); [same].

Wort im Mund umdrehen (jemandem das) *exp.* to twist someone's words • (lit); to twist the word in someone's mouth.

ORDER FORM ON BACK

Prices subject to change

AMERICAN	BOOK	CASSETTE
STREET TALK -1 . . . . *How to Speak and Understand American Slang*	$16.95	$12.50
STREET TALK -2 . . . . *Slang Used in Popular American Television Shows*	$16.95	$12.50
STREET TALK -3 . . . . *The Best of American Idioms*	$18.95	$12.50
BIZ TALK -1 . . . . *American Business Slang & Jargon* (general office • finance • meetings & negotiations • business travel • "computerese" • marketing & advertising)	$16.95	$12.50
BIZ TALK -2 . . . . *More American Business Slang & Jargon* (international trade • hotel & tourism • hospitality • real estate • human resources • management • "bureaucratese" • legalese • politics)	$16.95	$12.50
BLEEP! . . . . *A Guide to Popular American Obscenities*	$14.95	$12.50

FRENCH		
STREET FRENCH -1 . . . . *The Best of French Slang*	$15.95	$12.50
STREET FRENCH -2 . . . . *The Best of French Idioms (available September '96)*	$15.95	$12.50
STREET FRENCH -3 . . . . *The Best of Naughty French (available September '96)*	$15.95	$12.50

SPANISH		
STREET SPANISH . . . . *How to Speak and Understand Spanish Slang*	$15.95	$12.50

GERMAN		
STREET GERMAN -1 . . . . *The Best of German Idioms*	$16.95	$12.50

—— OPTIMA BOOKS Order Form ——

2820 Eighth Street · Berkeley, CA 94710

For U.S. and Canada, use our TOLL FREE FAX line: 1-800-515-8737
International orders FAX line: 510-848-8737 · Publisher direct: 510-848-8708

Name _____

(School/Company) _____

Street Address _____

City _____ State/Province _____ Postal Code _____

Country _____ Phone _____

Quantity	Title	Book or Cassette?	Price Each	Total Price

Total for Merchandise	
Sales Tax (California Residents Only)	
Shipping (See Below)	
ORDER TOTAL	

METHOD OF PAYMENT (check one)

☐ Check or Money Order   ☐ VISA   ☐ Master Card   ☐ American Express   ☐ Discover

(Money orders and personal checks must be in US funds and drawn on a US bank.)

Credit Card Number: **Card Expires:**

☐☐☐☐ ☐☐☐☐ ☐☐☐☐ ☐☐☐☐   ☐☐ ☐☐

Signature (important!):

SHIPPING

Domestic Orders: SURFACE MAIL (delivery time 5-7 days).
Add $5 shipping/handling for the first item · $1 for each additional item.
RUSH SERVICE available at extra charge.

International Orders: OVERSEAS SURFACE (delivery time 6-8 weeks).
Add $6 shipping/handling for the first item · $2 for each additional item.
OVERSEAS AIRMAIL available at extra charge.

SG1